Empowerment

Roger Cartwright

- Fast track route to mastering empowerment and releasing the full potential of all employees

- Covers the key areas of empowerment from understanding how to maximise employee potential and learning how to delegate, coach, and trust, to communicating vision and objectives and the role of the manager as a leader and empowerer

- Examples and lessons from some of the world's most successful businesses, including P&O, Mary Kay Cosmetics, Toyota and Marriott Hotels, and ideas from the smartest thinkers, including Kenneth Blanchard, David Logan, Kenneth Murrell, Tom Peters, and Robert E Quinn

- Includes a glossary of key concepts and a comprehensive resources guide.

LEADING

08.10

essential management thinking at your fingertips

Copyright © Capstone Publishing 2002

The right of Roger Cartwright to be identified as the author of this work has been asserted in accordance with the Copyright, Designs and Patents Act 1988

First published 2002 by
Capstone Publishing (a Wiley company)
8 Newtec Place
Magdalen Road
Oxford OX4 1RE
United Kingdom
http://www.capstoneideas.com

CIP catalogue records for this book are available from the British Library and the US Library of Congress

ISBN 1-84112-233-5

Printed and bound in Great Britain

This book is printed on acid-free paper

Substantial discounts on bulk quantities of Capstone books are available to corporations, professional associations and other organizations. Please contact Capstone for more details on +44 (0)1865 798 623 or (fax) +44 (0)1865 240 941 or (e-mail) info@wiley-capstone.co.uk

Contents

For reasons that will become apparent in Chapter 7, Empowerment Success Stories, this material is dedicated to those who lost their lives in the terrorist hijacking and attacks upon the World Trade Center in New York and the Pentagon in Washington, DC on September 11, 2001 and to the officers and crew of the liner Aurora (and shore-based staff) who worked so hard to bring us all home safely.

Introduction to ExpressExec

ExpressExec is 3 million words of the latest management thinking compiled into 10 modules. Each module contains 10 individual titles forming a comprehensive resource of current business practice written by leading practitioners in their field. From brand management to balanced scorecard, ExpressExec enables you to grasp the key concepts behind each subject and implement the theory immediately. Each of the 100 titles is available in print and electronic formats.

Through the ExpressExec.com Website you will discover that you can access the complete resource in a number of ways:

» printed books or e-books;
» e-content – PDF or XML (for licensed syndication) adding value to an intranet or Internet site;
» a corporate e-learning/knowledge management solution providing a cost-effective platform for developing skills and sharing knowledge within an organization;
» bespoke delivery – tailored solutions to solve your need.

Why not visit www.expressexec.com and register for free key management briefings, a monthly newsletter and interactive skills checklists. Share your ideas about ExpressExec and your thoughts about business today.

Please contact elound@wiley-capstone.co.uk for more information.

Introduction to Empowerment

This chapter considers:

» empowerment as the releasing of employee potential;
» empowerment as the three-way relationship between managers, their staff, and the organization;
» the need to adopt a less-controlling management philosophy to facilitate empowerment; and
» empowerment as a form of investment by the organization.

Writing in their 1999 text, *Empowering Employees*, Kenneth Murrell and Mimi Meredith make the point that empowerment appears recently to have become one of the most used words in management, but also one of the most misused concepts.

Whilst empowerment may create an idea of giving power to somebody, the concept is much more about the releasing of individual potential within the workforce and using that potential to the benefit of both the organization and the individual.

Modern management makes much of the concept of two-way communications. It is stressed, quite correctly, that effective communication includes a feedback loop (see the ExpressExec title on Communications). Empowerment also requires more than a single-track process. It is not just the empowerer who confers power onto a subordinate. There is, as will be shown in this material, a three-way relationship that comprises the empowerer, the empowered and the organization. This relationship needs to be in balance if there is to be maximum benefit to all three parties.

As will be demonstrated in Chapter 3 when considering the history and evolution of empowerment within the managerial process, empowerment can only begin to occur when management ceases to be a restrictive control function. Unfortunately it is only in recent years that many managers have begun to realize that their job is less about control and more concerned with coordination and facilitation. As the workforce becomes better educated and more sophisticated, control-type management becomes increasingly less appropriate. Empowerment is the process that can release and free up education and experience providing energy for work tasks that was previously being used, often unproductively, for control.

EMPOWERMENT AS AN INVESTMENT

The words trust, power, potential, support, and resources will be used throughout this material when discussing empowerment. Managers invest personal and corporate power, trust, and resources into individuals and groups in order to release a greater amount of "work" than the person or group might normally display. The purpose of this investment is to obtain something for, in effect, nothing, i.e. to make an investment that will pay back more than the original stake. Most people do not work to their full potential not through any form of laziness, but because the managers and the organizations that employ them do not know how to release that potential. Once they do, the difference in apparent ability can be enormous and well worth the initial investment.

Given that this investment can be so rewarding, why don't more managers practice empowerment? In part it may be ignorance, but for many managers the move from a controlling environment to an empowering one may be quite threatening. Do they really want empowered employees who may well question the way work is carried out? Unfortunately it is often the case that given unrealized potential, lower productivity but a quieter life over a dynamic organization brimming with ideas, many managers actually prefer the former – how sad for them, for their employees and for their stockholders.

What is Empowerment?

This chapter considers the following concepts related to empowerment.

» Empowerment is concerned with releasing the potential of employees to assume greater responsibility.
» Empowerment is a dynamic, three-way process.
» Delegation is not empowerment, but a step along the road to empowerment.
» Empowerment is a process rather than an event, although the latter may be held as a "rite of passage."
» The power available to individuals derives from a number of sources including personality, expertise, position, resources, relationships, and physical strength.
» Authority is the legitimate use of power.
» Delegation refers to the handing down of the responsibility and resources to carry out a task whilst retaining accountability.
» Accountability is the obligation to ensure that something is done, but does not mean that the accountable person has to actually do it.
» Responsibility is the obligation to do something as instructed or requested.

Simplistically it might be thought that empowerment is simply the act of imbuing somebody with the power to do something. In modern business, however, the situation is far more complex.

DEFINITIONS

Murrell and Meredith (see Chapters 8 and 9) have defined empowerment in terms of the enabling of someone to assume greater responsibility and authority through training, trust and emotional support. Responsibility and authority are covered later in this chapter, but it might also be appropriate to add both financial and physical resources to trust, training and emotional support.

Bill Ginnodo, editor of *The Power of Empowerment* (1997) sees empowerment as employees and managers solving problems that were traditionally reserved to higher levels of the organization.

Ken Blanchard, John P. Carlos and Alan Randolph, writing in 1999 under the title *The 3 Keys to Empowerment*, considered that the essence of empowerment lay in the knowledge, experience, and motivational power that is already in people, but is being severely underutilized. It would be a poor organization indeed that spent a fortune on a piece of equipment and then failed to use it to its full potential, but that is exactly what many organizations appear to do with the staff they employ.

Combining all of the above, a suitable definition of empowerment is:

"The process of releasing the full potential of employees in order for them to take on greater responsibility and authority in the decision-making process and providing the resources for this process to occur."

EVENTS AND PROCESSES

It is necessary to distinguish between an event and a process. In the early 1990s the UK company Autotype International, a coatings manufacturer based in Oxfordshire, undertook a systematic training program for supervisors. The culmination of the program required the participants to identify (individually) an issue within the organization and come up with a solution that included a consideration of costs etc.

One supervisor looked at the simple issue of protective gloves and the fact that these were discarded at each shift change despite the fact that rinsing them out would allow them to be used for three shifts before they became ineffective. The annual cost saving to the company if this were adopted would be around $20,000. The supervisor made a presentation to his peers and managers including the managing director. At the end of his presentation, the supervisor asked if he could implement the scheme. The managing director, who was impressed with the idea, replied surprisingly, "If this is so good, why hasn't it been done already? From now on I would rather you came to me to ask for forgiveness rather then permission." He then proceeded to wave his hand, deity-like, over the audience and announced that they were "now empowered!"

The act of telling somebody that they are empowered is nothing if it is not linked to a process of empowerment. The training that the supervisors mentioned above were undertaking was part of that process, a process that would continue if they were then supported in the decisions they then took. The actions of the managing director formed a rite of passage – a reference point in time that the supervisors could refer to when seeking resources, assistance etc.

POWER

It is also necessary to define what is meant by the term power. Power, as defined in the everyday world, is the resource that drives things. Anything that "gets something done" possesses this force known as power. Thus money can be a form of power, as can expertise, information and knowledge. Money, information, etc. are often referred to in management and business texts as resources, so it follows that power is a resource as well. Whilst there is often talk about the misuse of power, it must remembered that resources are neutral and it is up to the individual to decide how a resource is to be used.

Empowerment, therefore, must be something to do with the allocation of resources. Indeed, unless resources are provided, then empowerment becomes just an empty word.

As Helga Drummond has pointed out in her 1992 examination of the subject, power is dynamic and can never be either absolute or purely one way. A hermit may possess considerable potential power, but another person is needed for the power to be exerted. Power is in fact what drives influence, i.e. power is the resource that allows an individual or organization to influence another individual or organization to do something that the power source requires. In any application both parties are changed through the interaction, hence power can never be one-way or absolute.

The power of any individual within an organization is usually derived from a number of sources of power as described below, with perhaps one or two being the dominant power sources for that individual.

Physical power

Not perhaps the first thing that comes to mind when considering business issues, but physical power may well be a factor in certain law enforcement roles. Physical power does not necessarily mean sheer size, but is more a function of personality and confidence. The writer well remembers seeing a diminutive nurse calm down three hooligans in a hospital waiting room by her assertiveness (not aggression) and willpower. Physical power is not exerted because A is stronger than B, but by the fact that B believes that A is physically the stronger.

Personality power

Alluded to above, personality power, or charisma as it also called, has been the principal source of power for many well-known leaders. Richard Branson, Jesus Christ, Mohammed, Gandhi, Hitler, Kiam (of Remington fame) all possessed a certain something that made them stand out. Many others have it to a lesser extent, and the ability to use one's personality for the good of the organization, of others, and also of oneself is a most useful trait.

Expertise

In the modern, technological world expertise carries with it a great deal of power. The earnings that can be made by those who truly understand modern information and communication technology (ICT) systems give testimony to this. Expertise used to be based on experience; today it is experience plus knowledge that is all-important. Expert knowledge can confer considerable power on an individual, especially if he or she is working with those who have considerably less expertise in the particular field. One of the problems with expertise as a source of power is that it only requires one wrong call for credibility to fall quite rapidly. Expertise is also much more than just knowing the jargon – an expert who cannot make good on his or her words is eventually exposed as a charlatan.

Position power

Power can be gained just by a job title or even a uniform. If people believe that somebody has the authority to act in a certain way (see later in this chapter), they will assume that he or she also has had the necessary power conferred on them. How often do we question a person in a uniform that appears commensurate with the surroundings? Before the terrorist attacks of September 11, 2001 in the US, how many people would have questioned the authority of somebody in a pilot's uniform in an airport? Hindsight gives us 20/20 vision, but the answer is probably very few indeed. Much position power is conferred on people by their job titles or even job grade.

There is a common perception that somebody who has reached a certain position must possess the necessary skills and expertise in order to have been promoted. The "Peter Principle," first put forward by Dr L.J. Peter in 1969, suggests that promotion may occur past competence, i.e. promotion to the level of incompetence. People may be promoted past their optimum level and once in a new position it may be difficult to demote them. Position does not always indicate competence.

Resource power

There is a saying in English that "He/she who pays the piper calls the tune," a reference to the story of the Pied Piper of Hamelin. Resource power can often be exercised by those quite low down in the organization if they have control of a resource that is urgently needed. Much negotiation and bargaining at all levels of domestic, business and governmental levels revolves around resource power. "If you do or give me this (which I want), I will give you what you want," etc. The aim is to try to avoid a situation where there is a win/lose, lose/win, or lose/lose situation to one that is win/win, so nobody has to give away too much without receiving an adequate resource reward in return.

Relationship power

There is an old saying that is still often true today, "It's not what you know but who you know."

The importance of networking is stressed in nearly every business and self-development book. It is a fact that those close to the people who hold power are often seen as having a portion of that power themselves. Ask yourself a question: who is the second most powerful person in your organization? Often it is not the deputy CEO or deputy chair, but the PA or secretary to the CEO or chair. Persons who control access to the person with power often wield considerable power themselves. Gatekeepers have always been powerful figures.

Just being related to somebody with power may confer a degree of influence that is unwarranted. It is presumed by others that the relative will have extra influence or access the power figure. Relationship power is often irrational, but it can be a very potent force.

Other concepts that are important when considering empowerment are:

» authority
» delegation
» accountability
» responsibility.

Authority

Authority is the outward manifestation of power. It is a sign to others that the person or organization is sanctioned to act in a particular manner. Quite rightly, authority is normally given together with limitations on its use. These may be simple rules or as complex as the US Constitution, which defines the limits of authority of the Congress, the Supreme Court and the President.

Authority can be defined as the use of legitimate power.

As part of the empowerment process, the empowered needs to be provided with the authority to act and those who will be affected need to be informed that this person or organization has the authority to do certain things.

In the military, authority is often easy to spot as the badges of rank often signify increasing levels of authority. Thus commanders can issue orders to ensigns, but not to captains. There are often occasions, however, when expertise is held by a lower ranking individual and it is a wise senior who realizes that "with respect, Sir, I would reconsider that action" actually means "if you do that you will be acting very unwisely – Sir!" It is often the case that the more junior person has expertise power, whilst the senior may rely on position power.

Part of delegation involves the devolving not only of a task, but also the authority that is held by the delegator.

Delegation

Delegation is handing down responsibility together with the necessary resources and authority to somebody below one in the organization. However, unless the decision-making process also passes down the line, this is not empowerment, although it may be a step along the way to full empowerment – in effect, an interim stage. Under delegation, the delegator still remains accountable (see below) for the task and its manner of implementation. Accountability cannot be delegated.

Accountability

Accountability is the obligation to ensure that certain tasks are carried out. The accountable person does not have to carry out the task, but they will be held to account for it. Delegation, as described above, does not carry accountability with it, only responsibility. Accountability still rests with the delegator, who then makes the delegatee responsible.

Empowered staff carry both responsibility and accountability, or at least a share of the latter.

Responsibility

Responsibility is the obligation to actually carry out a task and thus can be delegated. There may have been no input into the initial decision-making process at all.

From the above it can be seen that the difference between empowerment and delegation is that the former has decision-making and accountability components that are lacking from the latter. As will be shown in both Chapters 3 and 6, the historical trend has been towards moving from delegation + control to empowerment + facilitation; approaches that require the use of very different managerial mindsets.

KEY LEARNING POINTS

» Empowerment is not so much an event as a transition process.

» Empowered individuals are involved in decision-making and accountability to a far greater extent than those to whom tasks are delegated.

» The aim of empowerment is the release of potential for the benefit of the organization.

» Individuals have a mixture of power sources that they can call upon.

» Authority is the legitimate use of power and has prescribed boundaries.

» Accountability cannot be delegated – once accountability is passed down, empowerment is taking place.

The Evolution of Empowerment

This chapter considers the following in relation to the evolution of empowerment.

» Empowerment has occurred in the social as well as the business environment.
» Empowerment becomes more possible as the general level of education rises.
» Human organizations have their roots in primate social systems.
» Organizations became larger as communications and transport became easier, necessitating the need for tighter control systems.
» If a manager believes that nobody likes work and will shirk responsibility, Theory X says they are likely to adopt a controlling style. Conversely, if the manager believes that work is an innate need and that people seek responsibility, Theory Y says they are more likely to adopt a facilitator style.
» Achievement, recognition and fulfilling potential are important motivators.
» Empowerment lies on a continuum that starts with true slavery.

The history of empowerment mirrors very closely changing social and educational norms. It is reasonable to assume that unless the workforce has received an adequate education, then the analytical skills required for decision-making may not be present and that empowerment is virtually impossible.

Once the workforce has a level of education that enables the individuals to analyze situations in an increasingly wider context, then if they are not empowered, frustration may well result.

The evolution of empowerment is closely linked to the ideas of management that have been in vogue since management became an occupation and an area for study in its own right with the growth of large organizations during the industrial revolution that commenced in the early 1800s.

Human beings, like other advanced primates, are social animals whose groupings have a distinct hierarchy and are territorial in nature. This affects the way humans design organizations and in the way the structures of those organizations are arranged to ensure effective management of people.

If the anthropologists such as Desmond Morris and Robert Ardrey are correct, then the development of organizational structures goes back beyond the evolution of humans to the very dawn of primate development. Living and working in groups with clearly defined membership, shared tasks, an agreed hierarchy and "space to call the group's own" (i.e. its territory) appears to be the natural form of primate social organization and it is thus not surprising that it is reflected in the structure of most work and social organizations. A recent text (2000) by Nigel Nicholson (a professor at the London Business School) entitled *Managing the Human Animal* makes interesting reading as he contrasts our current technological progress with social and behavioral norms that our Stone Age ancestors would recognize.

Up to the early 1800s most organizations were small because of the difficulty in communicating at speed over any distance. Paradoxically this led to greater empowerment of the favored representatives of rulers or merchants, as they had to act on their own initiative. Trust was very important. Widely diffuse organizations such as the Church, the Royal Navy and the great trading companies (the greatest of which was the Honourable East India Company) developed very clear hierarchical structures, that of the Church having survived for nearly two millennia relatively unchanged. Even when the Reformation led to the setting up of new Christian sects, these still tended to reflect to some degree the organizational structures of the Roman Catholic Church.

The structure of the Catholic Church has proved remarkably resilient. As far as human involvement is concerned, and meaning no disrespect, if we compare the Catholic Church to any other organization it has a CEO – the Pope at the head office in Rome; senior management both in Rome and at its principal branches (in other countries) – the cardinals; a set of branch managers – the parish priests; and even sales staff – missionaries. A similar structure is found in a traditional family with a clear hierarchy and promotion from within. Whilst the mission of any religious movement is spiritual rather than profit-oriented, the same structures that have proved useful for religious movements have also been adopted by business.

Leadership is also a key role in the way organizations develop and thus in the way staff are managed. One of Morris's observations in *The Human Zoo* concerns the similarity between leadership roles within primates including man. It appears that, as a species, we need leaders and leadership and that any organization without a clearly defined leader, even if just as a figurehead, is doomed to failure.

The earliest annals of military history show a command structure similar to that of today's highly technical armed forces – commander, senior officers, junior officers, NCOs, ordinary soldiers, sailors etc.

Because of the difficulties of communications, organizations were forced, in the main, to remain small. Those that did become large, such as the Church, Royal Navy, etc. mentioned earlier, set up quite complex communications systems for their time and developed extremely detailed operating instructions.

The Admiralty in London sent out dispatches to admirals and the captains of the ships under their flag. There was also a set of detailed fighting instructions telling each captain how a particular set of battle circumstances should be approached, in effect detailing the tactics a captain should use. If, like Nelson, the captain ignored the instructions and gained a victory, then little was said (although the instructions were rarely amended). If the captain ignored the instructions and suffered a defeat, then a court martial was the norm and possibly a severe punishment that could – and in the case of Admiral Byng in 1757 did – include execution! It should also be noted that if the captain obeyed the instructions to the letter and still lost the fight, they would also face a court martial and again severe penalties. As this writer pointed out when using the Admiralty as an example in his 2001 text *Mastering The Business Environment* (Palgrave, Basingstoke), their Lordships of the Board of Admiralty could not lose!

Once the railway began to develop, first in the UK and then in the rest of Europe and the US, communications were eased and it became possible to set up various branches of organizations in different towns. The removal of the need for workers to live with in immediate walking distance of their place of work meant that organizations could grow bigger without having to provide housing next to the workplace. This in turn led to the growth of management and supervision as a distinct work role. As more and more people began to be employed in any one organization, it became apparent that there was a limit to the number of individuals one person could supervise effectively. Urwick, writing in 1947, believed that the "span of control" was as few as one person supervising no more than five or six others. This was not a new concept, just an elucidation of something that had been recognized, especially by the military, for some time. Technology, as will be shown in the next chapter, has greatly increased the span of control and it might be more appropriate to talk of a span of influence to reflect modern business practice as regards empowerment.

The classic writers on management and supervision of the late nineteenth and early twentieth centuries, including Taylor (1911) and Fayol (1916), were considering organizations where there was not just a distinction between workers and management in terms of tasks, but also of education. They believed in the necessity for the same form of detailed operational instructions as covered earlier when discussing the fighting instructions of the Royal Navy. They believed that the uneducated workforce required tasks to be broken down into simple components. Workers were there to do, not to think. Fayol praised the idea of initiative, but only when shown by management. It must be remembered that there were at this time clear class distinctions in Europe and to a lesser degree in the US. Managers and workers did not talk save to give orders and report back. Social intercourse between these groups was virtually unknown.

Clearly, as educational standards rose in the Western world throughout the twentieth century, it became possible to loosen the span of control by allowing for initiative. This brought about a new component to organizational structure, that of the technicians. Technicians began to bring about their own empowerment through their technical expertise – a power source discussed in Chapter 2. This group of workers came to the fore as steam engines developed – they were the only people who could build and work these strange new contraptions. Managers were forced to seek their advice if the organization was to make the best use of the potential of new technologies. Technicians also brought forth a whole new training system, that of technical education. Whilst the older universities of the world, Oxford, Cambridge, Harvard, Yale, the Sorbonne, Heidelberg, etc. have their roots in classical education for the ruling classes, the Massachusetts Institute of Technology (MIT), CALTECH, the University of Manchester Institute of Science and Technology (UMIST), etc. are products of the rise of the technical and the need for specialized education.

MANAGEMENT BY CONTROL

Douglas McGregor, a US researcher, considered that there were two positions that managers could adopt when considering their workforce. The first position, which he named Theory X, held that:

» the average human being dislikes work and avoids working if at all possible;
» this dislike of work means that employees need to be controlled, directed and even threatened if necessary if the organization is to fulfill its objectives; and
» people require direction, but do not want responsibility.

In contrast, Theory Y held that:

» work is a natural human function;
» people relish responsibility;
» the rewards people seek are not only monetary; and

» the intellectual and creative potential of most employees is underutilized.

McGregor's point was that if a manager is an adherent to Theory X, he or she will probably be a controlling, directing, "cop" type of manager, whilst a manager who holds that Theory Y is nearer to reality is likely to adopt a more facilitating, empowering approach.

Theories X and Y were not put forward as examples of what is, but more as illustrations of the two poles of views held by managers in respect of their workers. As educational opportunities have increased it appears that Theory Y is closer to reality than Theory X. There are lazy individuals in any society, but in the main, work is a fruitful experience providing social interaction, achievement, and recognition in addition to monetary reward.

THE IMPORTANCE OF ACHIEVEMENT

Two of the most important writers on motivation, Abraham Maslow and Frederick Herzberg, have stressed the importance of achievement recognition, and what Maslow termed self-actualization, i.e. fulfilling one's own potential, as motivational factors. All of these are Theory Y traits and are not particularly amenable to management by control.

CATCHING IN OR OUT?

Whilst the concept of management being some form of police function still exists within some organizations, many managers have found that life is actually better if instead of going around trying to catch people out, they try to catch them in instead. Most workers are doing things correctly for most of the time, but in the old system it would be the few occasions when they did something wrong that brought them to the attention of management. Such an approach leads workers to try to cover up errors and thus organizational learning is stunted as more is learnt from things that go wrong than things that go right. In Chapter 7, as part of the Toyota case study, it will be shown how, if a mistake had been made, the worker and supervisor would jointly seek a solution that would prevent a recurrence. By allowing an error to be discussed without fear of punishment, learning could occur both for the individual worker and for the organization.

The idea that managers should move from a policing, controlling function to that of being a facilitator and coach has been a feature of the work of the US "management guru." In his various works, commencing with *In Search of Excellence* written with Bob Waterman, Tom Peters has stressed the need to facilitate the empowerment of the workforce in order to release the potential required for competitive advantage. One of the key areas that Peters has stressed is the role of the manager as a coach. The concept of coaching, whether in sport or business, is to achieve the maximum release of an individual's potential. It is a process, often over a long period of time, that requires a relationship of trust between the parties. David Logan and John King (2001) have shown how visionary managers are using coaching to empower people to unlock their full potential to the benefit of both the individual and the organization. They have pointed out that the diversity of having four generations within the workplace provides an opportunity for intergenerational learning. Above all, they stress the need for trust in this new relationship between managers and workers. They also stress the differences between training and coaching. The former is task-related whilst coaching centers on the individual and developing his or her potential.

Progressive organizations are now seeing that managers need to be trained and developed into their new role. It is no use just telling somebody that they are now a coach. Just as empowerment does not occur because of a pronouncement from senior management, neither will a culture of coaching. Many traditional managers may be deeply suspicious that releasing the potential of their subordinates may expose their own vulnerabilities. Sensitivity is required. Perhaps there is potential in the manager that is yet to be released? Who will work with the managers, and how, is an issue organizations embarking upon empowerment also need to consider.

RACE, GENDER AND THE GLASS CEILING

Racism, sexism, ageism, etc. are not just immoral and illegal in many jurisdictions, they are also bad business policy. It is quite amazing that there are still organizations in the developed world at the start of the twenty-first century that appear content to allow the potential of a significant part of their workforce to remain untapped.

Progress is being made, first through legislation and perhaps more importantly within organizations as senior management realize that no resource can remain underutilized. Writers such as Davidson, Cooper, Burke, Stith and Wirth have shown how the glass ceiling (the barrier to progression for certain groups) is being broken and how this benefits individuals, the organization and society in general.

That there are cultural differences between groups and that these may be manifested in different work ethics cannot be denied. However, as Fons Trompenaars, Harris and Moran and Richard Lewis have demonstrated, those managers who take the time and effort to understand cultural differences can use this knowledge to unlock potential and empower those who have been previously regarded in a negative light. The growth of female managers in India is testimony to the economic benefits that can be gained by moving forward from traditional stereotypes.

Meredith Belbin in the UK, best known for his work on team role theory, has linked his previous work to a consideration of gender. Belbin postulates that the technological changes over recent years have favored the further emancipation of women and that once organizations and societies recognize this, then tremendous potential can be released. The same arguments apply to different races. How much progress could mankind make if people were seen not as a race, color or creed but as a source of potential that can be released by empowerment?

The career of Pamela Thomas-Graham, CNBC president and CEO (the highest African American in the cable TV industry), as profiled by Robyn D. Clarke in the September 2001 edition of *Black Enterprise*, shows just how far potential can go when a person is empowered. Reading about this lady's achievements, it is clear that she is very talented. What a waste it would have been if that potential had remained unrealized and how frustrated might she have become.

CONTINUUM

Empowerment, like most managerial concepts, is not an absolute but a continuum. At the bottom end of the continuum is pure slavery – still, sadly, a feature of some regions of the world today. Wage slavery comes next, and at its bottom end it may be little different from pure slavery. One of the complaints about globalization has been the cutting of costs by employing third world contractors at less than subsistence wages. At the top end of wage slavery is the condition of many – dependence on a job where they have little decision-making power (but more than those in slavery), are still highly controlled by old-fashioned management systems, but with potential bottled up and either directed into hobbies or leading to frustration and stress. (See Fig. 3.1.)

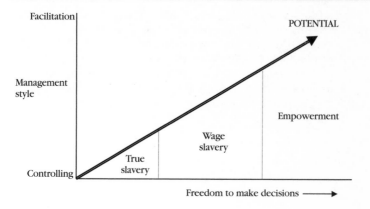

Fig. 3.1

Given that it is believed that we use only about 1% of our brain power, there seems to be an almost limitless potential, but is important to realize that freedom to make decisions outwith corporate guidelines and culture (see Chapter 6), and without a facilitating manager to coach, can lead to anarchy.

It may be difficult for an individual to say when he or she has actually become empowered. However, a consideration of the history of management from the industrial revolution onwards will show that both society and organizations have been empowering people in most regions of the world. Some are further ahead than others, but it is rapidly becoming realized that an empowered workforce is much more motivated and productive than one that is not so regarded.

KEY LEARNING POINTS

» Management styles have been moving from a concern for control to a requirement to facilitate.

» Managers now need to be facilitators and coaches rather then adopt a policing role.

» Catching people in is more fruitful than trying to catch them out.

» Racism and sexism have served to suppress potential, a situation that is both morally and managerially unacceptable.

» Empowerment is not a point in time, but an area along a continuum of freedom to make decisions.

» Managers may well not be natural coaches and need guidance in this role. They may also feel threatened if asked to unleash the potential of their staff.

Empowerment and the E-Dimension

This chapter covers the role of information and communication technology (ICT) in empowerment and includes:

- » ICT as an agent of empowerment;
- » new technologies as employment opportunities;
- » removing the tyrannies of place and distance;
- » education;
- » information handling;
- » communication;
- » disabilities;
- » negative aspects including privacy and communication overload; and
- » best practice case study – Stephen Hawking.

Paradoxically, developments in ICT have both accelerated and hindered the empowerment process. The ability to be free from physical, location constraints and to have access to effective communications and the wealth of information contained on the Internet has been a great boon to the empowerment process. At the same time, however, the ease of monitoring communications, the fact that managers can communicate globally in real time and the growth of surveillance and web cameras has meant that workers can be very closely controlled. Tracking technology can provide an organization with the instant position of its sales force and engineers, etc.

These developments have been so worrying that there have calls for them to be examined in terms of civil liberties and human rights legislation. ICT can destroy the right to privacy.

Both the positive and negative implications of ICT in respect of empowerment are covered below.

ICT AS AN AGENT OF EMPOWERMENT

ICT, used properly, can assist greatly in releasing potential in various areas, namely:

» new technologies
» removing the tyrannies of place and distance
» education
» information
» communication
» disabilities.

NEW TECHNOLOGIES

The rapid rise in computer-based technologies and applications from the 1980s onwards provided a huge opportunity for a generation of people who possessed the necessary aptitude and skills required to bring the products to the market place. Bill Gates of Microsoft, Stephen Jobs of Apple, and Jerry Yang of Yahoo! are just three of the names that have come to be associated with the computer revolution. Working from a small base, a series of household names have grown through the empowerment of talented staff. Dell, Microsoft, Apple, and Sun Microsystems are examples of organizations that have used the unleashing of the potential of often very young staff to achieve exceptional growth. Young people of considerable talent, who might well have been frustrated in a traditional organization, were able to find an outlet for their talents in an environment where they were valued and where traditional work practices did not always prevail.

Christopher Price makes the point in *The Internet Entrepreneurs* that some traditional methods were required to avoid anarchy. He describes how Netscape recruited the 51-year-old Jim Barkdale in 1995 in order to provide "adult supervision." Barkdale had a very successful corporate career with IBM, FedEx, and then as the number two at McGraw Cellular and provided the organizational knowledge that the entrepreneurs behind Netscape required. Having somebody like Barkdale on board empowered them to be creative rather than become engaged in administrative tasks.

REMOVING THE TYRANNIES OF PLACE AND DISTANCE

Prior to the development of railroads and streetcars, workers had to live next to their place of work. This alone limited the size of organizations. As transportation links grew, so did the distance away from work employees could live. The cost of prime site, city center property is now so high in major cities that many executives commute long distances to work each day with the resultant negative effects on performance, health and family life.

The use of video-conferencing, electronic mail and laptop computers together with advances in telephone technology has meant that it is no longer necessary for people to travel to the office every day. Home working, despite problems of isolation owing to lack of the social contact that ordinary working patterns provide, has increased in use. Technology has also enabled organizations to outsource work to other parts of the world, thus providing job opportunities (although there is the problem of home-based job losses). A great deal of data processing for US and European organizations is carried out in India where there are highly competent staff available in a lower wage rate economy. For the organization there is also the possibility of exploiting time zone differences to allow call center operations to be on a 24-hour basis without paying overtime.

The tyranny of place and distance often affected women in the workforce. Many have been forced to move locations as their partner's job changed. Many have also felt a need to remain at home whilst their children are young. Technology allows them to continue working from home if necessary, thus releasing their potential into the economy.

Whilst it is early days in analyzing the role of ICT in empowerment, the day cannot be far off where the location of a domicile will cease to be relevant when employing certain categories of staff and this will open up job opportunities to a much greater percentage of the global population.

EDUCATION

Education is a precursor to empowerment. ICT is revolutionizing the way in which education can be delivered. Distance is no longer an issue. Many colleges, universities and training organizations are using ICT to deliver educational programs to those who might otherwise find it difficult to attend regular classes. When the UK government instituted the Open University in the 1960s, those who had missed out as youngsters for personal or economic reasons were given a second chance. Facilitating lifelong learning is one of the ways governments and organizations can assist the empowerment process. The sheer process of undertaking degree level studies is horizon-broadening and mind-opening and it is this that leads people to see how far their potential may actually extend – usually much further than they first imagined. ICT is allowing education into the furthest reaches of the planet and bringing education and thus new ideas to more and more people each year.

There are some areas – the Taliban government of Afghanistan was an example at the start of the twenty-first century – that tried to inhibit the spread of education, especially for women. However, such attempts only mirrored those in the rest of the world in earlier times and every previous attempt to limit education to preserve a minority power base has failed. Education, like empowerment, is an unstoppable force.

INFORMATION

Murrell and Meredith in *Empowering Employees* demonstrate that processed information leads to knowledge and that shared knowledge becomes wisdom. Hence the importance of information not only as an organizational resource, but as a stepping stone to empowerment, because empowerment without wisdom is an empty vessel.

ICT has made the acquisition of information relatively easy. The Internet can be surfed using search engines and vast quantities of information obtained. Statistical analysis is also much quicker using computers. The downside is information overload. Part of wisdom and empowerment is knowing what information to act on and what to discard. The 80/20 rule is always worth bearing in mind: 80% of what is needed will be in 20% of the information. It may be enough to make a decision on 80% of the information. Eisenhower decided to launch D-Day on an 80% weather prediction given by Group Captain Stagg of the Royal Air Force. The only time that Eisenhower could have been certain of good weather on June 6, 1944 would have been at 0001 on June 7! Sometimes waiting for all the information possible means that an opportunity will have been lost.

The traditional rules about the validity of information apply to information gained from the Internet. First, it will only be a good as the person who put it there and they may have a particular bias. Information also needs to be checked for its currency, sample sizes, conflicting views etc.

COMMUNICATION

Prior to the development of railroads and the need for the electric telegraph to control train movements, the average speed of communication beyond line of sight was no more than about 10 miles per hour. As soon as electricity began to be used for communication purposes, the effective speed of communication jumped to that of the speed of light. Provided that the parties wishing to communicate possessed the right equipment and were linked by wire, they could communicate in real time. The empowering nature of these developments is not difficult to see. Information that cannot be acted upon is of no real use. The ability to communicate empowered those with the necessary equipment. Wireless technology empowered millions more as only the receiving and transmitting apparatus was required, as the technology dispensed (hence the name) with the need for a physical connection. No longer was it necessary to communicate from fixed points. The development of the mobile communication network that is characterized today by the cell phone had begun.

Linking telephone and computer technologies means the combination of information-gathering, the means of disseminating that information and the ability to confer for decision-making over large distances in real time. It used to be said that putting a wall between people cut communication by at least 60% whilst a stairway between them cut it by up to 90%. Modern technology overcomes these problems by making communication easier over distance and this in turn acts as an empowering force. Organizations are beginning to realize the strategic importance of their communication systems and many are making huge investments in such systems, especially as business becomes more and more global – the implications of which are discussed in the next chapter.

DISABILITIES

Perhaps one of the most dramatic examples of information and communication technology as an empowerment tool has been in the manner it has assisted many with disabilities into mainstream employment. Stephen Hawking, the professor of applied mathematics and physics and subject of the case study at the end of this chapter, is severely disabled with motor neurone disease (MND) and needs both a wheelchair and a speech synthesizer. The technology has not only empowered him to continue working, but also to produce the best selling *A Brief History of Time* as well as countless other books. Hawking's books have brought advanced physics and cosmology into mainstream debate – without the empowerment of modern technology, that would have been impossible.

Hopefully we are moving past the days when a disability meant that employment chances were almost non-existent. Voice recognition software, speech synthesizers, the ability to work from home and the ease of use of today's telephone and computer technology have all helped empower those with disabilities. Having a disability does not necessarily mean that mental capabilities are any less than those of the rest of the population. As the case of Hawking shows, what would the world have missed if technology had not been able to release his ideas and then disseminate them so that he was one of the most read scientists of all time? The empowerment possibilities that technology has provided for those with disabilities have been recognized by governments in the anti-discrimination legislation that has been passed in many jurisdictions. However, legislation can only go so far and organizations need to realize that these technologies can release potential for them by assisting those with disabilities to put their skills at the disposal of the organization.

NEGATIVE ASPECTS

Empowerment, as was shown in the previous chapter, is not encouraged in rigid, control-based management systems. Unfortunately ICT, whilst aiding empowerment as shown in the previous section, can also increase the degree of control managers can exert on staff.

Some control is always necessary in any situation, but too great a level of control can suppress initiative and acts as a counter-force to empowerment. Unfortunately there are still many managers who believe that their job is to police their staff rather than to coach and empower them.

ICT can be used negatively in a number of ways.

Invasion of privacy

Even as this material is being prepared in 2001, a debate is underway in the US, the UK, and other parts of Europe on the rights of employers to spy on their employees by using closed circuit television (CCTV) and reading electronic mail. A delicate balance has to be struck. In the UK, the government appeared to be seeking powers to intercept all electronic mail etc. if necessary. It is important that pedophiles, fraudsters and terrorists should not be able to communicate freely. It is equally right that organizations should be able to investigate fraud and theft etc. by employees. The issue, as yet unresolved, is where the line is drawn between what is an invasion of privacy and what is legitimate and reasonable action. It is likely that this debate will be fueled by the terrorist attacks on New York and Washington DC on September 11, 2001 and referred to in the second case study in Chapter 7.

Both the US and European Union have civil and human rights legislation that protects individuals. What changes will be needed to that legislation to balance the rights of the individual with the security of organizations and society in respect of the increased potential of communication systems remains to be seen, but the debate over the issue is likely to be both lively and contentious.

The current growth in CCTV and web cameras has given rise to concern that privacy is being totally eroded. Again, it is a question of balance. CCTV, by making the streets safer, may well be a factor for greater empowerment if it eases the security fears of people and allows them to move more freely.

Tracking

Linked in many ways to concerns about privacy, the use of tracking devices linked to global positioning systems (GPS) and computers can provide employers with instant access to the position of vehicles. Thus sales, delivery, and maintenance staff can be tracked on a constant basis. Is this intrusive? Some say yes, others claim it aids the efficiency of the organization by allowing routes to be tracked and vehicles to be deployed to meet needs. It all depends on how the resulting information is used. As long as employers accept that coffee and toilet breaks are a right, then all well and good.

The security implications are obvious. Stolen vehicles can be tracked and hopefully recovered.

Various countries have experimented with the electronic tagging of prisoners released on license. In many ways this is a form of empowerment, as it allows the individual to begin to achieve his or her potential in the wider world rather than being locked up.

Unnecessary communication

Electronic mail is sometimes too easy to use. The ability to send the same message to a large number of people simultaneously and with no extra effort than sending to a single individual often proves too much of a temptation.

Too much electronic mail is likely to result in important messages not receiving the priority they deserve in addition to causing information overload. It may also be tempting for control-centered managers to be constantly issuing instructions and demanding data to the detriment of the work that needs to be done.

As in all new developments, responsibility is required and the lead should come from management or else bad habits may seem to have some form of official approval.

Like all developments, the Internet and its associated technology are neutral. Whether it is used as a positive aid to empowerment or as a negative brake on releasing staff potential is in the hands of the managers of an organization. Used wisely, the vast amounts of information available and the speed of communication can help release tremendous individual potential.

BEST PRACTICE
Stephen Hawking

As mentioned earlier in this chapter, Stephen Hawking has become a best-selling author not in the usual genres of detective stories, murder mysteries, thrillers, romance, or science fiction but in the field of science fact–an area usually dominated by academic texts.

Hawking has a rare skill of making the deepest mysteries of the universe understandable by those with only a high school (or less) knowledge of physics. In 1997 this respected scientist wrote the foreword to *The Physics of Star Trek* by Lawrence Krauss (himself Ambrose Swasey Professor of Physics, Professor of Astronomy, and Chair of the Department of Physics at Case Western Reserve University in the US), written in response to the huge interest in science fiction/science fact that has developed alongside the popular Star Trek series of television programs and movies. That serious scientists such as these and science fiction can come together in this way is in part due to the role Hawking has played in making physics and cosmology so understandable.

In fact whilst Hawking has written a number of books for the general market in addition to learned scientific papers, he is not a writer by trade, but holds the Lucasian Chair of Mathematics (a post once held by Isaac Newton) in the Department of Applied Mathematics and Physics at Cambridge University, situated in the fenlands of England and one of the world's most renowned seats of learning.

Married with three children and one grandchild, Hawking would be an interesting subject for a case study purely on his ability to put forward complex ideas in an understandable format. He was one of the main contributors to the demonstration that Einstein's general theory of relativity pointed towards creation via the Big Bang and the forming of black holes. His academic qualifications include his PhD, 12 honorary degrees, fellowship of the Royal Society and membership of the US National Academy of Science. In 1982 he was made a Commander of the Order of the British Empire (CBE) by Her Majesty the Queen.

What is even more remarkable is that in another age, Hawking's brilliance might never have realized its potential. Born in 1942, he went to Oxford University and at the age of 21 was diagnosed as suffering from motor neurone disease (MND)/anyotropic lateral sclerosis (ALS).

By then, Hawking was undertaking postgraduate research at Cambridge and on the advice of his doctors he returned to his research, but with the knowledge that he had an incurable disease. Undaunted, he gained a fellowship at Gonville and Caius (pronounced Keys) College and married Jane Wilde. Jane Hawking, as she is now known, is the author of *Music to Move the Stars – a Life with Stephen*, published in 1999.

By 1974 they had three children but by 1980, Stephen was requiring more and more nursing care and when he caught pneumonia in 1985 it was only by performing a tracheotomy that his life was saved.

One of the symptoms of Hawking's condition is slurred speech and the operation removed his power of speech altogether. Hawking had been in a wheelchair for some time. Thus by 1985, one of the world's most brilliant minds was trapped inside a body that could hardly move and now communication could only be achieved by the raising of an eyebrow.

How was it, then, that Hawking was able to write the best-selling *Brief History of Time* in 1988?

A computer expert named Walt Woltosz from the US sent Hawking a computer program he had written, called Equalizer. The program allowed Hawking to choose words from a series of menus on the screen, by pressing a switch in his hand. The program could also be controlled by a switch, operated by head or eye movement – unremarkable by today's standards, but revolutionary in the 1980s. David Mason, of Cambridge Adaptive Communication, fitted a small portable computer and a speech synthesizer to Hawking's wheelchair, providing him with mobile communications. This allowed him to communicate at up to 15 words per minute, either spoken or downloaded to the computer. Hawking puts a large part of his success down to the quality of the speech synthesizer, which was developed by Speech Plus. He makes the point that those with slurred speech are often treated as though they have a mental handicap when it is purely a speech problem and nothing to do with their intellect. Hawking's complaint is that he now has a US accent!

In the case of Stephen Hawking, technology has empowered him not only to have a working life and a happy family relationship. By releasing the potential he has inside of him into the books and seminars that are presented to the public it has allowed one of the great minds of the age to articulate complex ideas to a global audience despite a crippling disability. The empowerment potential of information and communication technology is exemplified through the continuing story of Stephen Hawking.

KEY LEARNING POINTS

» Information and communication technology can aid or hinder empowerment depending on how it is used.

» ICT can help overcome problems of distance and location that prevent many from fulfilling their potential. It may be especially useful for those groups who have not received a fair deal in the employment market.
» The educational potential of ICT to aid empowerment is huge.
» As shown by the example of Stephen Hawking, ICT can provide empowerment to many with disabilities.

The Global Implications of Empowerment

This chapter considers the global implications of empowerment including:

- » the global marketplace;
- » globalization;
- » growth and empowerment;
- » the effect of the empowerment of the global customer;
- » global education and empowerment;
- » the need to take account of cultural norms when embarking upon an empowerment process; and
- » best practice – Marriott Hotels.

Globalization is defined by Ellwood (2001) as:

">... a new word that describes an old process: the integration of the global economy that began in earnest with the launch of the European colonial era five centuries ago. But [sic] the process has accelerated over the past quarter century with the explosion of computer technology, the dismantling of trade barriers and the expanding political and economic power of multinational corporations."

The above quote, which is also the starting quote for the ExpressExec title Going Global, might sound like a subject for economists, politicians and social scientists but of what relevance is it in a series such as ExpressExec and to a consideration of empowerment?

More and more organizations are reaching out to a wider, more global marketplace to a large part as a result of the developments in Internet, computer and telephone technology. As this process increases in pace, then an understanding of how globalization may affect business and the requirements of senior management to become global rather than local leaders is becoming a prerequisite as part of the strategy for an increasing number of organizations. As organizations become ever larger and their component parts separated by oceans and continents, so there is a requirement for staff to be empowered to make decisions based on local rather than home-based conditions. The concept of a traditional span of control as introduced in Chapter 3 becomes less and less applicable as organizations grow ever larger. Rather than try to control everything from the center, a much better strategy is to ensure that those working in the various regions are well versed in the organizational philosophy and systems and then to empower them to act as local circumstances dictate, provided that this does not run counter to overall policy.

One of the problems that is claimed is behind the riots and disturbances at recent meetings of world leaders is a perceived belief by some, mainly but not exclusively to the left of the political spectrum, that globalization was somehow replacing democracy with government by commercial organization or pan-regional governments.

Whilst Ellwood (quoted earlier) states that it was Europeans who began the globalization process, today they have been joined by organizations from other parts of the world. US organizations Ford, General Motors, Coca-Cola, IBM, Wal-Mart, Boeing, and Microsoft are just some of the larger players and from the Far East Sony, Hyundai, Mitsubishi, Mitsui, and Toyota have joined Imperial Chemical Industries (ICI) and P&O from the UK, Royal Dutch Shell from the Netherlands and Airbus Industrie, the pan-European commercial aircraft manufacturer.

It is salutary to note that according to the 1999 UN *Human Development Report*, the total sales in 1997 of General Motors, Ford and Mitsui were each greater than the gross domestic product (GDP) of Saudi Arabia – an oil-rich country (sales in $US: General Motors – $163bn, Ford – $147bn, Mitsui – $145bn; GDP of Saudi Arabia – $140bn). Many multinational companies are now richer than whole countries and it is their economic power that has given rise to concerns about the process of globalization.

GROWTH AND EMPOWERMENT

Organizations usually begin on a small local basis. As the staff numbers are usually small, communications tend to be easy and informal. Such organizations often empower staff without knowing it. As the atmosphere may be more like that of a family, there is often encouragement to involve subordinates in the decision-making process. As the UK writer Charles Handy (1976/78) has shown, it is only when organizations begin to grow that they develop a more formalized culture with rules and a hierarchy that can begin to stifle empowerment. (See Fig 5.1.)

There reaches a point, however, when the organization, like most living organisms, is too big to function as a single entity controlled by one brain. It can become a "society" coordinated by a central authority.

What tends to happen is that the organization grows by either acquiring subsidiary operations or developing them from its original core businesses. These subsidiaries, whilst being controlled by the parent company, will have their own hierarchies and thus a degree of organizational empowerment. They are expected to contribute financially and report to the parent whilst coordinating their activities with other members of the group, but they are likely to have at least

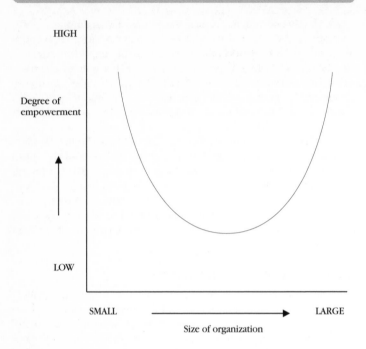

HIGH

Degree of
empowerment

LOW

SMALL ⟶ LARGE

Size of organization

Fig. 5.1

some degree of autonomy and thus empowerment. It is often the case that the subsidiaries are the repositories of local knowledge and are empowered to use this knowledge to the benefit of the group as a whole.

Apart from size, one of the reasons that organizations have had to empower staff has been the advent of a new phenomenon brought on by the Internet and the ease of transport across the globe – the empowered global consumer.

THE EMPOWERED GLOBAL CONSUMER

There used to be a time, as recently as the 1960s and 1970s, that a vacation abroad meant the opportunity to not only see new sights and experience different cultures, but also to purchase products that one could not find at home. The same products now appear in stores from Sydney to Springfield and from Tokyo to Topeka. The same music fills the air and the same fashions adorn the bodies. The whole world seems to use the same software applications on PCs that vary little from country to country. It is this commonality throughout the world that so worries the opponents of globalization who claim that traditions and heritage are being lost as everybody adopts a seemingly Western lifestyle fueled by Western advertising.

In fact, they should be less worried than they appear because it is only in commerce that true commonality appear to have a basis. In other aspects of life, humans appear to be as diverse as ever.

In the modern world the smallest retailer or manufacturer with a modem can reach across the globe and thus, access to particular products and services is restricted not by barriers of distance or geography, but only by the access customers have to the Internet, access that is growing daily. Software, music products and even the ExpressExec series can be delivered electronically (with safeguards to protect copyright and intellectual property). However, consumers still consider a degree of diversity attractive and often require local adaptations to global products. Indeed, achieving the required local diversity at a low cost may be the key to success for many organizations as they can then offer what the world wants with the diversity that the local requires. Doing this requires local staff to make local decisions. Decision-making as near as possible to the point of product or service delivery (i.e. the customer) has been a basic tenet of customer service literature and training in recent years. This requires staff empowered to make decisions. A customer in Paris cannot wait for a company headquarters in Singapore to rule on a particular deal. He or she will expect local managers to have the power to make such decisions. Hence globalization leads to empowerment as an almost natural process.

Many global organizations realize that there also needs to be a commonality of quality and service and thus empowerment is granted, but within the overall policy guidelines of the company. McDonald's, one of the great global fast food brands, has very strict standardized quality systems but serves beer in Germany, though not in the UK.

Local managers can introduce local variations after consultation with corporate headquarters.

The best practice case study at the end of this chapter is on Marriott Hotels, a company that has grown internationally by empowering its staff.

GLOBAL EDUCATION AND EMPOWERMENT

The role of education as an important facilitator of empowerment has already been stressed in this material. A commitment to education by the vast majority of the world's nations and the development of information and communication technology, especially the Internet, is assisting in the opening up of educational access across the globe.

The world's more entrepreneurial colleges and universities have been quick to realize the extra dimension that the Internet can bring to distance and open learning in reaching larger numbers of potential students. The technology provides a far greater degree of interaction between institution and student and between students than is possible in a print- and mail-based education system. These developments have been evolutionary rather than revolutionary. Australia was a pioneer in using the radio to provide elementary education to remote areas, whilst the Open University in the UK used television, radio, and print media for undergraduate studies from the late 1960s onwards. Today, whole programs can be taken via the Internet, making high quality higher education and the empowerment that it provides available to increasingly large numbers of potential students.

Without the analytical skills and intellectual development that education brings in addition to knowledge, empowerment cannot be anything other than superficial. Once people are educated to a high level, they begin to demand empowerment so that they can fulfill their potential. Education and empowerment are irrevocably linked and form two sides of a dynamic triangle, of which organizational commitment – to be covered in the next chapter – is the third.

CULTURE

Culture, often defined as "the way we do things around here," is very important to empowerment. The threat that empowerment of subordinates may pose for their managers has already been mentioned in this material and will be covered again in the next chapter. Empowerment may also present challenges to a whole culture or society.

The glass ceiling that has prevented women and minority groups from attaining the high profile positions many of them deserve has also been covered earlier. There is still a glass ceiling in the US and much of the so-called "West", but it is often nothing when compared to the social and employment position of women in other parts of the world. There are areas where women are denied work and even education; the Taliban regime in Afghanistan was strongly criticized at the end of the last and the beginning of this century in this respect.

In other areas, promotion is less a function of ability as of time served or even age. Empowered younger employees may be resented in such a system.

Those seeking to empower employees in another culture need to take great care they are sensitive to the cultural norms. Trompenaars, Lewis, and Harris and Moran have written at length about the difficulties and methods for conducting business affairs in other cultures and are well worth consulting before attempting to implement an empowerment program. Even if a culture is not geared to the empowerment of certain groups, this does not mean that the status quo has to be accepted. Cultures are dynamic and do change, albeit slowly. It does mean, however, that care and sensitivity are needed.

Fons Trompenaars has been one of the foremost writers in considering the implications of cultural differences for global operations. As he makes clear, there is great potential in empowering workers with different cultural norms, but only if it is done in a sensitive manner that recognizes both the workers' cultural norms and needs and those of the organization. By a careful study of how a particular culture does things, the organization can adapt its policies to make the best of the skills in that culture. Every culture has particular strengths and empowerment is about building on strengths.

Empowerment may not mean the same in different cultures and managers need to ensure that they are on the same wavelength as their employees whom they are trying to empower. Some cultures are much more hierarchical than others and whilst this may seem to add extra reporting layers, it may be important for social cohesion. Other cultures may not readily accept the empowerment of minority groups or women. As stated earlier this does not mean empowerment should cease – only that it be handled carefully and sensitively.

THE DIVIDED WORLD

Commentators often refer to the world as being divided between the haves and the have-nots. Perhaps a fairer description might be that there are the empowered and the non-empowered. Many of the critics of the growth of globalization claim that the process does little to increase the prosperity of workers in developing countries or empower them, but only serves to increase profits for the global organizations. They point to the rise of terrorism on a global scale as being a symptom of the lack of empowerment and a feeling of helplessness amongst the unempowered. Not surprisingly, there are those who claim that the horrific events of September 11, 2001 in New York and Washington DC were a result of a feeling of frustration and lack of empowerment by certain groups. This book is not the place for such a discussion. The writer's view is that the prime suspect in the attacks as a multi-millionaire could hardly claim to be unempowered and that the attacks were political, not economic. Nevertheless, there are large areas of the world where there is resentment of Western wealth and a perception of exploitation. Exploitation is taking without giving back. Empowerment through education and the raising of educational, health and social standards on a global basis may give the terrorists less of an excuse to carry out their murderous business.

BEST PRACTICE
Marriott Hotels

One of the issues in managing a chain of global hotels is that customers expect a consistency of standard across any particular brand and they also want instant action to remedy any problems or difficulties. With guests staying perhaps for only one night, there is little time for discussion and checking back with corporate HQ; staff on the spot need to be free to make very quick decisions.

The global operation of Marriott had humble beginnings in the opening of a root beer stand on 14th Street in Washington DC in

1927 by the 26-year-old, newly married J. Willard Marriott. Later that year, the name Hot Shoppe was adopted when the stand started to serve food and again in 1927 Marriott opened a drive-in Hot Shoppe, also in Washington DC.

Whilst the drive-in operation showed Marriott's flair for grasping opportunities, in this case the beginnings of mass automobile ownership, his next venture was even more entrepreneurial. In 1937 he pioneered in-flight catering for Eastern, American and Capital Airlines. This operation was based on Washington DC's original airport – Hoover Airfield – now the site of the Pentagon. By 1939 he was also servicing government cafeterias, a profitable venture given the huge expansion of government activities during the war years.

Staying in the Washington DC area, Marriott opened his first hotel, the Twin Bridges Marriott Motor Hotel in Arlington, VA in 1957. Although this was to be the start of a major global hotel chain, Marriott-Hot Shoppe (as the company was re-titled in 1964) continued in the fast food business, buying up other operations and becoming international in 1964 with the acquisition of an airline catering operation in Venezuela.

Another name change in 1967 saw the Hot Shoppe title dropped and the company becoming the Marriott Corporation. By the 1980s Marriott was the largest operator of airport catering in the US, had expanded into timeshare vacations, had increased the number of hotels owned and in 1985, a few months after J. Willard Marriott passed away, acquired the Howard Johnson operation. J.W. Marriott Jnr was by then chairman of the board. The Howard Johnson hotels were sold, but the restaurants etc. remained.

The 1980s and 1990s saw a massive expansion of the Marriott Hotel operation in different price segments by both new building and acquisition. By 1998 the company was reporting sales in excess of $12bn and comprised 1,500 hotels across the world, a figure that rose to 2,000 just a year after the last Hot Shoppe closed.

Two thousand hotels require considerable coordination, but managing them across the globe requires empowered staff. These staff need to understand the philosophy, policies and culture of Marriott, the needs of their customers and the importance of consistency. J. Willard Marriott was a firm believer in listening to his staff. His son has reported that his father believed that people gave of their best when they knew that their views were important. Part of the company philosophy is that it is not in the hotel business, it is in the people business and people includes both staff and customers. Many of the P&O guests stranded in New York after September 11, 2001 (see Chapter 7) were staying at the Marriott Marquis on Broadway (just by Times Square) and have spoken of how helpful and concerned the staff were with their plight. Just as one might expect, one might think, but it is worth remembering that New York was under terrorist attack at the time and the staff might have been excused for thinking a little more about their own plight. The writer was at the hotel the previous day and can verify the excellent customer service he received when trying to send a facsimile to the UK. There was a problem with sending the facsimile and the front desk clerk took ownership of the problem by saying, "you go back to your room and I'll make sure this goes, there's no need to wait. I'll let you know when it has been sent."

Most of the Marriott hotels are franchise operations, including Whitbread Hotels in the UK and Ritz-Carlton. Nowhere is the balance between control of standards and empowerment more important than in a franchise. In these operations the franchisee is gaining the Marriott name and the commitment of the franchisor not as an employee but as a partner. J.W. Marriott Jnr has written of the need to ensure that the center does not exert undue control on franchisees. He reports of a case where an individual's wages could not be increased without permission. Whilst it would not do for a franchisee to be far out of line with company policy, in the case of an outstanding individual a modest rise should be agreed locally.

Marriott have devised an empowerment program for employees that sets out quite clearly the boundaries of decision-making for each individual Marriott associate, as the company likes to entitle its staff. Marriott is rightly proud of its standard operating procedures (SOPs), but these deal only with common issues. The company does not believe that consistency equals rigidity. SOPs are there to allow the staff the time to deal with the uncommon events that occur and that is where they are empowered to act on their initiative and sort things out for the guest. It is how difficulties are handled that customers usually remember.

The key to the Marriott success is contained in the previous paragraph; a consistently high standard applied according to the company's SOPs does not, and should not inhibit individual enterprise. If employees know that empowerment is one of the organization's core values, then will not be afraid to act decisively knowing that provided they have remained within the corporate philosophy, they will receive support.

KEY LEARNING POINTS

» Small organizations often feature empowered staff because of the close-knit relationships.
» Large organizations need to empower staff as a result of physical distances between sites.
» Global operations require empowered staff who can react to local needs.
» Education and empowerment are irrevocably linked.
» Cultural norms must always be considered before embarking on an empowerment program.
» Consistency does not have to be equated with rigidity.

Empowerment – the State of the Art

This chapter considers current views and practices on empowerment with reference to:

» the key elements to empowerment;
» the commitment of the organization, managers and staff;
» the importance of goals and norms;
» the facilitating and leadership role of managers;
» the need for an enterprise rather than a blame culture;
» trust and its importance to empowerment;
» the role of the team; and
» human energy.

THE KEY ELEMENTS OF EMPOWERMENT

In the previous chapter it was stated that empowerment is part of a triangle with the three sides being:

» empowerment;
» education; and
» organizational commitment.

On their own, each of the above is meaningless. Empowered people (or pseudo-empowered people in this instance) without education and experience will not have the skills to make effective decisions, however committed the organization is. If the organization is not fully committed to empowerment then the whole exercise is likely to be just rhetoric and have no substance, a state of affairs that leads to frustration.

Empowerment depends upon:

» a committed organization;
» committed employees;
» clear goals and norms;
» facilitating managers;
» a culture of enterprise rather than blame; and
» trust between all parties.

A committed organization

When Tom Peters and Bob Waterman published *In Search of Excellence* in 1982, they introduced a new way of thinking to management. Building on the work of Fiedler (1964), they demonstrated practical examples of what is known as contingency theory. Previous views of management had sought to find a "one right way to manage;" contingency theory states that there is no one way to manage, but a series of styles etc. that managers can adopt contingent upon the situation. Thus, whilst shouting out orders may not be the usual method of managing a highly motivated and well-trained staff, there are times when it is the right thing to do. A fire in the building is a good example: managers should not instigate a discussion at such moments.

Max Hastings and Simon Jenkins have recorded the experience of a Royal Navy warship captain during the 1982 Falklands conflict between the UK and Argentina. As the captain pointed out, whilst discussion and involving everybody in decisions was applicable to normal peacetime management, it was less suited to war conditions. In a crisis and as the bombs began to fall, the captain started shouting out orders. This was what everybody wanted – an authority figure to take instant decisions. They did not want to sit around debating whether a move to starboard or to port was the right answer – they would have been sunk long before a decision was reached. After the action, however, it was right and proper for the captain to gather those involved together regardless of rank to discuss what happened and how performance might be improved. Some things can never be delegated and command of a warship is one of them, hence the importance of trust, to be covered later in this chapter. As one sailor remarked in conversation with the writer of this material, "there is no need to like your officers, but you do have to trust them!"

Tom Peters has gone on to write a large number of books on the subject of excellence, quality and getting the most out of people (see Chapter 8). In *In Search of Excellence*, Peters and Waterman introduced a series of attributes for excellent companies, three of which are particularly appropriate in a consideration of empowerment.

Productivity through people

It is people who get things done. Behind every useful machine is a human being programming or operating it. Organizations that do not look after their people may be successful in the short term, but will end up losing good employees to organizations that have a more people-oriented attitude. Empowered people are an asset because they are able to be more effective and are usually better motivated. The more control a person has over a task, the more efficiently they are likely to carry it out. As the Toyota case study in Chapter 7 points out, the best people to carry out quality assurance are the people actually making the product. If they are empowered and have pride in their work, they have a vested interest that goes far beyond wage remuneration to ensure quality.

Autonomy and entrepreneurship

Peters and Waterman demonstrated that those organizations that provided staff with a degree of autonomy within corporate guidelines appeared more successful than those operating strict controls on staff initiative. Companies such as Lockheed with their famous "skunk works" operations and Apple with the development of the Macintosh have been able to tap into the innate entrepreneurism of employees to produce new products that have astounded the world. However, controls are necessary, as demonstrated below.

Simultaneous loose–tight properties

An interesting term but a very important one. Whatever happens within an organization should be in accordance with the goals and norms of that organization. Peters and Waterman found that in excellent organizations, the boundaries on autonomy were very clearly defined – the tennis court principle: when the ball is in, everything is OK, but if it crosses the line, the point is lost. Culture, quality standards, and financial controls should be tight. Initiative and decision-making can then be subject to empowerment within the guidelines. Once the rules are clearly known, staff can then be empowered to act knowing that they have the support of the organization.

Without the commitment of the organization, empowerment cannot happen. As will be shown below, managers have to buy in to the empowerment principle and employees need confidence and security to accept being empowered. Ultimately, much depends on trust.

Committed employees

Given that recognition and achievement have been shown to be important motivators, it might be expected that all employees would welcome empowerment. However, this is often not the case.

Given that the concept of empowering employees is relatively new with many organizations only just beginning to move away from strict controls, it is not surprising that employees might be suspicious.

The kind of quotes one obtains when talking to employees about their suspicions are:

"It's management's job to manage, not ours."
"I just work here, they're paid to make decisions."
"I suppose this means more work for no more pay."

"Who takes the blame if it goes wrong?"

"I'm not qualified."

One cannot blame people who have been subject to strict controls and a blame culture (see later) for thinking this way. Empowerment is more than just an administrative and skills process, it is also a hearts and minds process. The words of a certain US official *do not* apply! (The official is reputed to have remarked, when asked about a hearts and minds campaign during the Vietnam War, "when you've got them by the b**ls, their hearts and minds will follow.") The opposite is true. Despite years of oppression, the East German people never really took communism to their hearts and when the Berlin Wall came down, the way the communist philosophy disappeared from the East German people was spectacular.

People cannot be forced to be empowered, nor will just telling them that they are empowered be enough. Empowerment is very much a state of mind and an attitude. To assist the process of buying in to empowerment, the organization needs to ensure that the final four items in this section are given careful attention. Once employees feel secure with the commitment of the organization to empowerment as a shared idea and not a way of imposing on staff, they are likely to be much more amenable to its concepts.

Clear goals and norms

It is impossible for people to make effective decisions unless they are very clear about the context within which those decisions will be implemented. If empowerment is to be effective, the organization must ensure that all concerned understand the goals of the organization and the norms to which it operates. As covered earlier, these norms act like the boundary lines on a tennis court. They give a clear indication of the scope of decision-making power and an indication of when it is necessary to seek higher authority.

An understanding of what the organization is seeking to achieve is an important motivational factor and provides the framework around which empowerment can occur. It is difficult for staff to feel secure with empowerment if they are unsure of where the boundaries of their authority actually are.

Facilitating managers

The threat the empowerment of staff can present to managers has already been mentioned and should never be underestimated. Whilst staff may often perceive that their boss is secure, the truth is that many managers worry about their own abilities. It should be a task of every manager to assist and coach his or her staff, but unfortunately too many neglect this area of managerial responsibility.

The manager as a coach is a very important part of empowerment. Logan and King have addressed this issue in *The Coaching Revolution*. They quote from experience at Marriott Hotels (see previous chapter) of how effective a manager who adopts a coaching role can be. Like many coaches in sport, coach/managers may see their protégés overtake them in ability. This should not be a threat, as most people who succeed never forget who their mentors were. Organizations appreciate managers who can bring people on.

Another key managerial role is to ensure that the empowered receive not just authority, but have access to all the resources required to make and implement decisions. A manager's role is to facilitate resources, not to hold them back without very good reason.

Those wishing to introduce empowerment will need to ensure that the managers of the organization are on board first. Empowerment that is accepted by senior management and the workforce but only has lip service paid to it by middle management is doomed to failure.

A culture of enterprise rather than blame

A blame culture can rarely be one that encourages empowerment. In a blame culture, people are far too busy covering a certain part of their anatomy (CYA) to wish to make decisions for which they may then be punished. The whole concept of catching people in rather than out is to encourage decision-making. Mistakes will occur and it is the role of the manager to work in partnership with the responsible persons (see Chapter 2) to find out what went wrong, why it went wrong and how can it be avoided in future.

If people feel that mistakes lead to punishment, then they will try to cover them up and the opportunity to find a solution will be lost.

The above does not mean that empowerment is a soft action. Mistakes that occur by going beyond the guidelines are a different matter. Empowerment carries with it rights and responsibilities and one of the major responsibilities is knowing when to say "no, that is beyond my authority or remit." This is not inflexibility provided that the guidelines are sufficiently broad in the first place.

One of the benefits of empowerment is that the employees begin to act as their own control mechanism. They are often far harder on themselves than senior management might be. This does not cause problems, as the employees have ownership of the issues.

Trust between all parties

The final requirement in this section is that the parties need to trust each other. Employees need to know that empowerment is good both for the organization and themselves. Blame cultures (see above) need to be eliminated and managers should be assisted to move from facilitation to control. Trust is never one-way: it always has to be reciprocated. Once there is trust, true empowerment can take place and the full potential of the staff can be employed in fulfilling the goals of the organization.

HOW EMPOWERING ORGANIZATIONS BEHAVE

Those organizations that have moved towards empowerment show certain characteristics that are less evident in control-based organizations. Spreitzer and Quinn (2001) of the University of Michigan Business School have described the five disciplines required to using empowerment to set free employee potential. They have categorized these as:

1 empowering the person who matters most;
2 continuous vision and challenge;
3 continuous support and security;
4 continuous openness and trust; and
5 continuous guidance and control.

Control has been an area that previous sections of this text have suggested should be relaxed. However, there always has to be some form of control or there is chaos. The key to control is that it is not fixed. A person learning to drive may do so in a dual-control vehicle, moving to a normal vehicle as they gain confidence. A newly qualified surgeon will work under the control and guidance of a senior colleague until his or her competence is deemed such that close supervision is no longer required. Empowerment is about relaxing control as competence grows and not sticking rigidly to control systems that inhibit potential rather than release it. The management skill is knowing when to exert control and when to release it. In many ways, this is very much like the role of a parent. A good parent or manager will ensure that the offspring/employee has all the skills and knowledge required and will then back away to allow potential to be displayed.

The person who matters most, according to Spreitzer and Quinn, is actually the person doing the empowering. This person is going to have to display leadership skills and to do that needs to be empowered him- or herself. Self-knowledge is a key to effective leadership. Knowing who we are and, importantly, what our strengths and limitations are empowers us. A manager who knows where he or she is going tends to instill confidence in staff. However, if he or she does not show that they have concern for the development of their staff potential, they may find that those under them regard them with suspicion. There will be an absence of trust, as staff perceive that all their hard work is going into somebody else's career plan. In an empowered organization, everybody's career plan is assisted.

Spreitzer and Quinn also stress the need for support and trust as covered earlier in this chapter. They also consider the importance of vision. Vision is key to any successful organization. However, vision should not be purely confined to senior management. Vision (i.e. what the organization is and where it is going) needs to permeate the whole organization, not as a trite mission statement but as a living thing that is not only known but is understood by everybody. Once people understand the vision, they can see their role in achieving it.

The final comment to be made on the work of Spreitzer and Quinn is their distinction between mechanistic and organic empowerment. Whilst the vision for the organization usually comes from the top, a top down approach to other concepts such as delegation, rewards, and task-setting is very mechanistic. An organic approach is more concerned with understanding the needs of the employees (the writer would also add understanding the needs of the customers as well), producing a model for empowered behavior, using team building to encourage cooperation, encouraging intelligent and considered risk-taking, and then trusting people to perform.

As was shown in the case study on Marriott Hotels in the last chapter, standard operating procedures (SOPs) cannot dictate how the unusual is dealt with and it is an organic approach to empowerment that enables people to take decisions in this area.

Many managers will feel more comfortable with mechanistic empowerment as it shows that they are doing something to empower the workforce, but on their own terms and with retention of control. Organic risk-taking may be more of a threat, but the rewards for all concerned can be much greater as it is more likely to release the potential of the managers in addition to the employees.

MANAGERS AS LEADERS/TEAMS AS EMPOWERERS

Many authorities have seen empowerment as more of a leadership than a managerial role. It could be argued that in a business situation, the ability to empower is what transforms a manager into a leader.

Blanchard, Carlos and Randolph (see Chapter 8) stress the leadership aspects of empowerment. They make the point that too many managers (including many who think that they are leaders) believe that all they have to do to empower people is to give people the authority to make decisions. The process, as has been shown, is very much more complex than that. A true leader will provide differential empowerment to meet the skills and aptitude of the individual. He or she will also ensure that all the training and resources required for authority to be exercised are in place.

Empowerment alters the way we have traditionally thought of leadership. It is noteworthy that in his work on team roles, Meredith Belbin does not have a team role dedicated to the leader. He talks about coordinators and shapers, but recognizes that leadership can migrate according to the circumstances. There is also a considerable difference between titular and actual leaders. Barrie Pitt, in an analysis of the events in France and Belgium in 1918, makes the point that the German army had an interesting structure. The titular army group leader would probably be from the royal family, but all he really did was attend to parades. His chief of staff, a professional army officer, was the real leader, issuing orders over the titular leader's name. Many organizations have seats of power that do not appear on the organization chart.

Coaching is a leadership trait. Effective leaders should work closely with those who have potential to release it. Part of the leadership skill mix is the ability to recognize potential and develop it through empowerment.

Belbin's work is of especial interest to empowerment. Belbin contends that maximum efficiency occurs through the synergy of a well-constructed team. He has postulated nine specific team role types that need to be present in a team for this synergy to occur. This does not mean that teams should consist of nine people, as most of us have two or three quite natural team roles. The roles are those of:

» Coordinator (previously referred to as chairman or woman)
» Resource Investigator
» Plant (the creative role)
» Team Worker (concerned with the internal dynamics of the team)
» Shaper (the challenging role)
» Implementer
» Completer-Finisher
» Monitor-Evaluator
» Specialist.

Each role has its strengths and, importantly, an allowable weakness; the opposite side of a positive strength. Belbin makes the point that removing an allowable weakness may also undermine the strength associated with it. For example, Shapers can be rude and short-tempered. However, they are also energetic and challenging – very useful in a crisis. Make them behave according to company rules and they will do so, but what use is a polite Shaper who is no longer prepared to challenge?

What Belbin and others have shown is that a knowledge of team roles actually acts so as to promote empowerment. This knowledge can provide a person not only with knowledge about the behavior of his or her colleagues and employees, but also self-knowledge. Knowing that some weaknesses are allowable can be a relief. Knowing also that there are natural roles and roles that the person is not suited to is very liberating. The writer is a Shaper, Plant and Resource Investigator, but scores very low as a Completer-Finisher. Unfortunately, he has no eye for detail. However this material has been put together with the assistance of a proofreader – usually these people have high Completer-Finisher tendencies. Without such people the writer might never have work published. Knowing the limitation forces the seeking out of complementary people, and this can empower all concerned to become involved in something that they would eschew as an individual owing to a lack of skills and aptitude.

A supportive team can do a great deal to boost confidence and thus empower an individual.

CREATING HUMAN ENERGY

According to the laws of physics, it is impossible to get something for nothing. Even if we burn a piece of wood we have found in a field, the heat energy released is not free – it was paid for not by us, but by years of sunlight etc. If an organization wishes to empower staff and release their latent potential and energy, then as shown throughout this chapter, it needs to put things in place itself. What is released is more than the organization has put in because it is the result of the synergy between the individual's previous experiences, education, upbringing, and training in addition to the work the organization has undertaken.

In an amusing but perceptive book entitled *Zapp!: The Lightning of Empowerment*, Dr William C Byham and Jeff Cox take the reader on a metaphorical journey through the operations of the Normal Company in Normalburg USA. The hero is Ralph Rosco. The company was formed many years ago by Norman Normal to manufacture the "Normalator."

The key point of the book is that Ralph had potential and yet the company never released it, and when he had a good idea nobody would listen, as it wasn't their job to initiate change. *Zapp* is well worth reading to see how Ralph becomes empowered using something entitled Zapp. Humorous certainly, but with a serious message, *Zapp* is well worth studying for anybody involved with empowerment who wishes to release human energy.

Many managers are amazed to find that their employees are known in their communities for other things. They may be excellent musicians, preachers, mechanics, gardeners, handymen, butterfly collectors, model railroaders etc. At work they may appear dull and unmotivated.

Their energy is not directed to the organization: they only do as much as they need to collect their pay. Whose fault is this? The talent is there, the energy for outside activities exist. Could it be that they are empowered outwith work and receive more than money - recognition and achievement perhaps? Should the organization not be deflecting some of that energy towards its goals through empowerment?

KEY LEARNING POINTS

» There is a link between empowerment, education and organizational commitment.

» Unless the organization, the managers and the employees are committed to empowerment, it is unlikely to occur.

» There will be times when strict controls and orders are required - this is the contingency approach.

» Productivity through people, autonomy and entrepreneurship, and simultaneous loose-tight properties as described by Peters and Waterman are important organizational considerations when contemplating empowerment.

» Empowerment works best when employees are aware of the organizational vision, goals, and norms.

» Under normal circumstances, managers should facilitate rather than control if empowerment is to prosper.

» Blame cultures inhibit empowerment.

» Trust is a vital ingredient in empowerment.

» Team support and team roles have an important empowering effect.

Empowerment Success Stories

This chapter contains three case studies on organizations that have demonstrated success in empowering employees. Two of the three, Mary Kay (a US-based cosmetics operation) and Toyota (a Japanese/global automobile manufacturer) are straightforward examples of good organizational practice. The other case study started as a consideration of the role empowerment plays in the entertainment industry (a multi-billion dollar global industry). Whilst researching this subject with the assistance of Phil Raymond, the cruise director on one of the latest UK superliners, other events intervened and the writer was able to experience the empowerment of the staff of Phil Raymond's employers (the UK operator P&O Cruises) at first hand. That case study is more personal than the others for reasons that will become obvious.

CASE 1: MARY KAY

With the concept that P&L is "people and love" rather than "profit and loss," Mary Kay the company follows the philosophy of its founder, Mary Kay Ash. Since 1963, Mary Kay, Inc. has grown from a sales force of 11 to one numbering well over 750,000. Mary Kay does business in 37 markets on five continents and upward of $1.2bn in wholesale sales worldwide. Mary Kay® also consistently ranks among the best-selling brands of facial skin care and color cosmetics in the US as well as offering cosmetics for the male customer – a rapidly expanding market.

Born in Texas, Mary Kay Ash (or Wagner – her maiden name) has known tragedy, having had to bring up three children on her own through bereavement. Whilst originally planning to be a physician, she showed an aptitude for selling, and this is the direction her career took. She retired in 1963 after 25 years at World Gifts. One of the things she had noted was the glass ceiling effect (see Chapter 3) as male colleagues were promoted ahead of her despite her superior abilities.

As she was an energetic sales person, her retirement lasted only one month, and she began to write a career book for women. This turned into the idea of a company that was for women and run by women. She obtained the formula for a skin care cream and, with the assistance of her husband and friends acting as beauty consultants, the new company, Beauty by Mary Kay, began to take shape.

One month before the scheduled launch of the new venture her husband died but, undeterred, the company started operations on the auspicious date of Friday, September 13, 1963.

Whilst Mary Kay wanted the company to be profitable, her main goal was the empowerment and enrichment of women's lives through recognition, motivation, support and, of course, the opportunities to have their own income. For nearly four decades, Mary Kay Inc. has been considered one of the finest business opportunities for women, with many of its independent national sales directors earning career commissions in excess of $1mn.

Allied to the commercial side of the enterprise is the Mary Kay Ash Charitable Foundation which contributes both to cancer research, particularly cancers affecting women, and to the prevention of violence against women.

In order to empower women in the 1960s, Mary Kay had to adopt flexible working practices that took account of family life. A great many organizations (but by no means all) recognize this today, but in the 1960s it was quite revolutionary. The company was also one of the earliest proponents of the "selling party" made famous by Tupperware. The parties allowed women to both socialize and buy. They also provided new recruits for the organization.

Mary Kay operates on the principle that to receive you have to give and the more you give, the greater the rewards are. The empowerment philosophy goes to the core of the company and some examples of the philosophy are shown below.

» *Consultants are not isolated*. All consultants and sales directors share their experience and guidance with new team members until each reaches her potential, a classic example of empowerment at work.

» *No territories*. In Mary Kay's "adoptee" program, consultants attract new consultants from any location they choose – in their hometown, while on vacation or while traveling. The local sales director then takes new team members under her wing, while eligible commissions return to the original recruiter. This is very different from the way other types of organization selling in the same manner operate.

» *No-pressure sales*. Mary Kay skin care is taught, not sold. Hard sell would be unlikely to produce repeat business and would certainly harm the empowering image of the company. Consultants operate with the goal of helping women achieve positive self-image and of leaving the customer feeling better about herself.

» *No competition*. Consultants are recognized and rewarded not for competing against others, but for competing against themselves. Consultants earn rewards for beating their own records not somebody else's. This has the advantage that a newcomer can look at her previous records and try to beat them rather than trying to match the sales of an experienced colleague.

» *God first, family second, career third*. According to Mary Kay's philosophy, a career is not considered an end in itself, but a means to an end; to personal fulfillment, family comfort and harmony; to a balanced life; to self-expression. Perhaps many of those suffering work-related stress might do well to ponder the above.

» *Financial opportunity*. Each consultant operates as an independent businessperson who can choose to operate her business according to a pace and schedule that works best for her individual life, with no limits on her ability to earn and progress in her Mary Kay career. Thus those working for Mary Kay are really working for themselves.

» *Personal development and fulfillment*. Working in the Mary Kay environment is about more than money. It is also about self-confidence, self-esteem and self-respect. Mary Kay wants all women to use their God-given talent to become better than they are.

The IPO for the company was in 1968 and by 1972 sales had reached the $18mn level with the distinctive pink trucks becoming a familiar sight on US highways. Annual growth up to 1978 was an average of 28% and by 1984 over half of the employees were women, with a third of the consultants combining their Mary Kay activities with other jobs.

A downturn in 1985 led to Mary Kay Ash organizing a leveraged buyout in order to reorganize the company.

Mary Kay now operates a worldwide operation with 1991 retail sales being over $1bn and in 1992 the company made its Fortune 500 debut. As the time line (below) shows, expansion into new markets has been a key strategy in recent years.

TIME LINE FOR MARY KAY

» 1963: Company formed on Friday, September 13.
» 1964: Products for men introduced.
» 1968: IPO.
» 1969: Company begins to manufacture its own products.
» 1971: First international subsidiary in Australia.
» 1978: Canadian subsidiary opens.
» 1979: First consultant to earn $1mn.
» 1980: Argentine subsidiary opens.
» 1985: Company returned to family ownership.
» 1989: Company ceases testing on animals.
» 1991: Retail sales exceed $1bn.
» 1995: Mary Kay now in 24 markets including China and Russia.
» 1996: Mary Kay Ash Charitable Foundation set up.

» 1999: Markets now number 31.
» 2000: 50% of orders via the Internet.

KEY INSIGHTS

» The glass ceiling is irrational as women can do just as well as men.
» Arranging work patterns and work delivery to suit employees is empowering.
» An empowerment philosophy must permeate the whole organization.
» A successful business can also be a socially responsive one.
» Empowered people compete against themselves rather than against others.

CASE 2: ENTERTAINMENT AND EMPOWERMENT, PHIL RAYMOND AND THE *AURORA*

The second of these empowerment success stories was intended to be a fairly straightforward account of the importance of empowerment within the field of live entertainment. Those responsible for the organization of live entertainment such as Phil Raymond, a well-respected senior cruise director working for the UK operation of the global P&O Princess Cruise operation (currently the number three player in the global cruise market) rely on the professionalism of entertainers. Once a live show has started, the producer can no longer take control and needs to have complete faith that the performers will behave as they should. There have been well-documented occasions, especially on live chat shows, when such faith has proved to be misplaced.

The operational functions of operators within the global cruise industry have appeared in other ExpressExec volumes, notably *Managing Diversity*, *Creating the Entrepreneurial Organization*, *Going Global* (where a profile of the P&O Princess operation is provided) and *Managing Hypergrowth*. Given the rapid growth enjoyed by the cruise segment of the tourism industry throughout the latter years of the twentieth century it is little wonder that so many of the major players feature in cases on success. However, the aim of using Phil Raymond's methods of operation was less connected with the sector and more with the importance of setting boundaries and then empowering people, as discussed in the earlier chapters of this material. Fate, however, intervened in a dramatic fashion and placed this writer in a situation where the empowerment of staff became clearly apparent. The 76,000 Gross Registered Tonne MV *Aurora* is a UK-flagged vessel operating in the UK cruise market, usually out of Southampton. The UK market comprised approximately 750,000 customers in 1999 out of a global total of 9.5 million, making it the third largest market after the US (6.25 million) and Asia (800,000).

Phil Raymond in his "entertainment" guise is a typical example of the variety/game show host. A "cheeky chappy" with a catch phrase of "the night is still young and you are?" – hopefully the audience will yell back the fact that they are still beautiful – he strikes a distinctive pose in a series of jackets that are eclectic to say the least. Phil Raymond is a typical variety entertainer, good with people and possessing a stage presence.

Phil's sea-going career began when he was booked as a singer/impressionist to appear on the Chandris liner, *Australis*, in 1977 bound from the UK to Australia. Paid off in Australia and forced to find his own way home, he signed back on board as a member of the general entertainment staff responsible for organizing deck games, quizzes and bingo.

Having joined P&O in 1982, Phil has risen to be a senior cruise director. As in many service industries, this type of role has grown in importance over the years. Even airlines now recognize the importance of the senior staff member in the cabin in ensuring a good customer experience and thus repeat business. This in no way detracts from the importance of the captain of the ship or aircraft, but the average passenger will interact far more frequently with the cruise director and his or her staff than with the captain. The entertainment can make or break a cruise experience for many, hence the importance of the cruise director role. The cruise director has a major internal public relations role and this means that he or she needs to perform a balancing act between being a performer and also a senior member of management. In many ways it is a case of wearing different hats – or in Phil's case, jackets. As mentioned earlier, Phil often dresses in a flamboyant manner when on stage, but also presents the image of a very competent manager when he appears in uniform blazer around the ship dealing with problems and answering queries. This is a point that will be picked up later in this case study when referring to events in Boston, MA on September 15, 2001.

The entertainment personnel on a ship such as the *Aurora* fall into four basic categories. There is a small team directly under Phil Raymond who put together events and manage the entertainment aspects of the cruise. There is the technical staff responsible for sound, lighting etc. Ship-board entertainments have progressed far beyond the small orchestra that gallantly played as the *Titanic* foundered in 1912 and the vast majority of modern cruise ships are equipped with the technology to stage full production shows. There is often an in-house or contracted general entertainment team of singers and dancers, and finally there are guest artistes ranging from cabaret performers to major names from the world of showbiz. P&O have a competitive advantage in the cruise industry in that as they operate brands separately dedicated to the US, UK, German and Australian markets it is possible to ensure that the entertainment is culturally in tune with the vast majority of passengers – especially important where humor is concerned, as many comedy acts tend to be nationally specific in their material.

Such a diverse group must be empowered. The entertainment is live and those providing it are living in direct contact with their audience. A bad performance one night and a passenger might well tell the performer about it the next day. As the entertainment is an integral part of the vacation package it is not unusual for members of the audience to walk out midway if they are unhappy about something or think they might be better entertained elsewhere on the ship. It is doubtful whether those who had paid for a Broadway show would be as inclined to leave in such a manner.

Cruise directors such as Phil Raymond have to earn the respect of entertainers and lay down clear guidelines as to what can and cannot be done and then rely on the entertainer to interpret those guidelines within the ambience of their act. Certain comedy subjects are usually taboo – seasickness being one of them (unless referred to obliquely). The age and experience range of the audiences can be very large and thus material needs to be middle of the road. Special late night cabaret spots provide for more adult entertainment – all other material must be clean.

Acts are booked by the shore office, but advice is taken from cruise directors who try to see new acts on land before recommending them for a cruise venue. Performing at sea in close contact with the audience on a day-to-day basis is not for those entertainers who value their privacy.

Phil Raymond's approach to empowerment is a customer-focused one. He encourages his staff to empathize with the customer and to go the extra mile for them. Repeat business is highly important to the P&O Princess operation and the company needs customers who will remember the extra input from staff and who will tell their friends. He also believes in a robust reporting and appraisal system that allows him to discuss what went right and what was not so good about a show or event. His philosophy is learning, not punishment (although he has the sanction of recommending removal from the ship if necessary). New staff are "buddied" by more experienced team members. The UK operation is fortunate in that many of the staff have been with the fleet for some time and are thus known to the repeat passengers, to whom they can introduce newcomers. There is considerable in-house training and a camaraderie that allows staff to discuss ideas freely. Passengers do not want a standardized product for their entertainment. Jamie's quizzes on the *Aurora* are different from those conducted by Emma. Both are good but it is the individuals who make the difference and add variety. That an individual approach can be taken in an overall standardized quality context is at the heart of empowerment. Staff know where the boundaries are and that they are free to work within them. In a tennis analogy, Phil Raymond only has to be a cop when the ball is out and even then, the performer etc. knows that the ball was out. It only when there is a dispute that the umpire role comes into play.

That should have been the meat of this case study.

However, the 2001 highlight for many "addicted" UK cruisers (and *Aurora* can carry as high as 80% repeat customers) was to be the vessel's maiden entry into New York, where she was to undertake two three-day corporate charters before returning to the UK. Of the 1700+

passengers who sailed on her out of Southampton, some would return by air on the day the ship arrived in New York, some would undertake independent or P&O-organized tours and then fly back or return on a leisurely sea crossing, whilst others would join by air and just sail back. This was less of a cruise and more of a traditional Atlantic crossing as in the 1920s and 30s. These facts would be of little importance in a series on business were it not for the fact that the *Aurora* made her US landfall at Boston, stayed overnight and then spent an afternoon and a night sailing past Long Island to arrive in Manhattan on Sunday September 9, 2001.

By the morning of September 11, with the exception of those passengers who had left New York by air on the 9th, there were a large number of P&O customers either in New York or Washington, DC, whilst others were en route to Eastern Canada or New England on tours. A large party were actually in the Arlington National Cemetery when the US was struck by a series of devastating terrorist attacks that left over 6000 civilians, military, and emergency personnel dead, destroyed the twin towers of the World Trade Center in New York and blew a large hole in the home of the US Department of Defense – the Pentagon – in Washington, DC.

The writer was fairly close to the Pentagon that morning and could not fail to be unnerved by the media reports from Washington itself, New York and Pennsylvania (where another hijacked airliner had crashed) that spoke of not if, but when, the next attack would be delivered and the fear that weapons of mass destruction (chemical, biological or nuclear) might have been involved.

Those whose view of the US in particular and the West in general had been derived from the television or movies might have expected panic, but one of the manifestations of an empowered people is their ability to behave rationally in times of crisis. People were streaming over the George Taft Bridge in DC by foot and by vehicle, but they were not fleeing. The police were in control and there was no sign of panic. Nowhere were there the scenes of vehicles banging into each other as their occupants sought their personal safety at any cost. People were helping each other.

Whoever was responsible for this attack (and it is not in the remit of this series to comment) failed in their intention within seconds of the attack, as it did not bring the US to its knees. All they really achieved is exactly what Admiral Yamamoto (a most perceptive leader and analyst) warned the Japanese Government of when he was ordered to attack Pearl Harbor in 1941. They went up to a tiger and stood on its tail – a foolish act if ever there was one.

Those who have derided Western methods of democracy, education and management as being in some way shallow and without foundations will have to re-think their views. Throughout that day one saw ordinary people doing things for others not because they were told or ordered to, but because they lived and worked in a system that has empowered its members to take initiative and responsibility.

Watching President George W Bush address the nation that evening, the writer was struck by the lack of visible anger and the steely Churchillian resolve shown by the US citizens crowded into a bar/diner not a mile from the White House – another sign that the attack was really a dismal failure. He remarked to a man next to him that it was difficult for a foreigner to know how to respond (even if that foreigner has worked in the US and served briefly with its military).

On finding that the writer was from the UK, the man made a remark that will stay with this writer for a long time:

"Hell, you're no foreigner – you guys are family. We know you'll stand by us."

So it proved, as the UK prime minister announced within hours of the attack that Britain would stand shoulder to shoulder with the US and there were few dry eyes, British or American, in a hotel bar a few days after the attack when the guard at Buckingham Palace played "The Star Spangled Banner" on the orders of Her Majesty the Queen. Given that the words relate to a little unpleasantness between the US and the UK in 1812, it was all the more poignant.

It is at moments of crisis that the true nature of empowerment is shown. Telephone communications between the US and the UK were overloaded. The *Aurora* was at sea and most of the customers were scattered across the Eastern seaboards of the US and Canada with some at the very heart of the attacks.

It is only since returning to the UK that the efforts put in by P&O staff to ascertain the whereabouts and safety of the passengers has become apparent. In one case the company prevailed upon a hotel operator to have a room opened to check if the final two people had actually slept in. They were, in fact, on Staten Island and unable to return to Manhattan. The writer and his partner had not undertaken the organized excursion in Washington, DC, that day and returned to the hotel in the afternoon to find an anxious tour guide stationed in the foyer trying to account for his last two "charges."

By September 12, the company had ascertained that thankfully none of the passengers or crew on leave had been killed or injured and used technology to set up a UK emergency telephone call center and information on the corporate Website informing relatives that their loved ones were safe. By September 14 (only three days after the attack) the company had put into place all of its contingency plans. These affected not just the *Aurora*, but also the *Royal Princess*, which had docked in New York on September 10, and the *Pacific Princess*, actually operating out of New York on Bermuda Cruises.

Hotels in New York and Washington, DC, had been prevailed upon to keep rooms for those passengers who were stranded. Passengers due to fly out were given full refunds. Those who could not fly back would be accommodated on board *Aurora* and whilst the return trip might take 10 days, they would be sure of reaching home safely. Assistance was provided in contacting employers as a number of passengers were worried about not turning up for work as planned. Not surprisingly, of all those spoken to who had this concern, not one employer said anything other than "all that matters is that you're safe – just get back in one piece."

Aurora's program was to have been to leave New York on September 15, visiting Newport, RI, Boston, MA and Bar Harbor before setting off across the Atlantic for a September 25 arrival in Southampton.

With the need to pick up stranded passengers in Canada and to embark crew and entertainers to replace those who had flown back on September 9, the program was amended to a Boston departure on September 15 followed by a day at sea to allow everybody some rest with a visit to Bar Harbor on September 17 and Halifax, Nova Scotia on the next day in order to pick up the remaining complement. New York harbor being closed, *Aurora* had berthed at Boston's Army terminal to discharge her first charter (the second being canceled). These new arrangements were released as a press statement and a note to passengers on September 14. Much effort had to be put into establishing communications with those traveling independently, but the systems appear to have worked.

It was a long bus journey for many on September 15. The party that had been down as far as Richmond had a 500+ mile journey up to Boston. 1500+ passengers began to arrive in the afternoon of the 15th into a port where security was considerably more severe than it had been when *Aurora* had first arrived en route for New York. Coaches were unloaded one at a time. Passports received careful scrutiny, as did baggage. Nevertheless it was a welcoming site after a 10-hour bus trip to see *Aurora* waiting, lights blazing and with the Red Ensign of the UK Merchant Marine and a courtesy Stars and Stripes, both at half staff. Nearby were two other cruise liners, hastily diverted to Boston, making the port seem much more crowded than usual.

Sailing days are usually fraught for the staff and times of happiness and anticipation for the passengers. This was not like any sailing day the writer had experienced. There was no doubt that whilst all were relieved to be back "home" as some now referred to the ship, there were those who had been very near to the heart of the attacks who were in a state of tension and anxiety. Recognizing this, P&O arranged for two of the their chaplains to fly out to Halifax to join the ship and offer comfort to those who required it.

Embarkation had none of the fun that is usually associated with such an event. The horrific death toll was only just becoming apparent. Phil Raymond's entertainment staff were fulfilling an important role that day. Dressed in blazers and white skirts or trousers they presented an air of authority as they assisted in embarkation and security procedures. As Phil pointed out, it is at times of crisis when empowerment comes to the fore. They did not have to be told how to behave to match the new circumstances – it came naturally. Body language and dress can be very important when dealing with difficult situations. The authority that the entertainment staff generated added to ease the process. Many of the passengers had never experienced such high levels of security. A high security state can be threatening in itself. Whilst for some it may give reassurance, it can also act as a reminder of what has and may yet happen. One cannot order staff to appear calm and authoritative. One can only train and empower them.

One thing remarked on by many was of the welcome they received back on board. The fixed smile for the customer is well known, but the welcome back received on board *Aurora* was very genuine. Staff were glad to see their customers back safe and sound and fell over themselves to provide extra little kindnesses and service. It appears that these were spontaneous and not planned. The company knows that they can rely on an empowered staff to act as circumstances dictate. Common sense was shown. Many of the crew knew the writer well. On staggering aboard over 12 hours since leaving a hotel in Southern Pennsylvania, he was greeted and then asked "do you need somebody to show you up to your cabin?" Even though there had been a cabin change, he knew the way and was able to relieve a steward of the chore of escorting him, thus making that staff member available for somebody less familiar with the ship.

The embarkation and sailing from Boston after the events of the previous week could have been very unsettling. Thanks to a staff who knew what to do and when to do it, it was as pleasant as possible under the circumstances. The entertainment staff had been briefed on the coping cycle and how to react to passengers in distress. The day at sea to unwind was an excellent idea, as was the choice of the first number by the singer (actually the theater director as the guest artistes were not able to join until Halifax) at the show that night. He chose "Give my regards to Broadway" as a tribute to the city and people of New York. It was just the right touch.

With the exception of the tail end of Hurricane Gabrielle that passed to the North, the trip home was uneventful. However, when the tip of Lizard Point in the South West of England emerged out of the mist on the afternoon of September 24 this writer, for one, felt a huge weight drop away.

As an incidental, 18 hours into her maiden voyage in 2000, *Aurora* suffered a seizure of a main bearing. The resultant press reports and customer comments, far from being negative, praised the crew and the company for the way they dealt with the problem. Passengers received a full refund and a free cruise.

(If the above case is unlike any other in this material or indeed this series, the writer makes no apology. Empowerment can often be best seen best in adversity. One hopes that the like of September 11, 2001 will never be seen again but it was felt important to record how a great nation and one particular organization dealt with a very difficult situation and how the resolution of the problems were, in the end, down to the competence of an empowered staff. If you were in New York or Washington, DC that morning, you might also understand the need to write about it.)

TIME LINE FOR PHIL RAYMOND, THE *AURORA*, AND THE ATTACK ON THE US

- » 1950: Born Haywards Heath, West Sussex, UK.
- » 1965: Left school. Trained and qualified in hairdressing, but continued outside work singing with a local band and performing with local drama group.
- » 1971: Joined Butlin's holiday camps as a "Redcoat" entertainer, Scotland.
- » 1972: Worked in clubs in England and on television.
- » 1977: Appointed by Chandris Lines as an artiste on the SS Australis. Paid off in Australia and worked his passage back to UK as an assistant cruise director plus a weekly cabaret.
- » 1979: Opened an entertainment agency in Folkestone and managed three top night-clubs/discos.
- » 1981: Appointed as cruise director for Fred Olsen Lines Black Watch.
- » 1982: Appointed cruise director for P&O, working on Canberra and Victoria/Sea Princess.
- » 1997: Canberra's final season, the ship arriving in Southampton to emotional scenes in September. Joined the Arcadia.
- » 1999: Appointed as cruise director of P&O's new flagship, *Aurora*, then building in Germany.
- » 2000: *Aurora's* maiden voyage, May 1. Voyage terminated owing to mechanical defect.
- » Sept 1, 2001: *Aurora* leaves Southampton, UK with approximately 1,700 passengers.

» Sept 7: *Aurora* arrives Boston, MA.

» Sept 8: Midday, *Aurora* leaves Boston.

» Sept 9: *Aurora* arrives New York in the early morning. Passengers disembark for tours or flight to UK. Charter group embarks.

» Sept 11: Four US aircraft hijacked. World Trade Center destroyed, Pentagon damaged.

» Sept 12: P&O ascertain whereabouts of all passengers and put out press release and notice on corporate Website. *Aurora* docks at the Army Terminal in Boston, MA.

» Sept 13: Day of mourning in US. Many *Aurora* passengers display Stars and Stripes and wear national colors.

» Sept 15: Booked and stranded passengers rejoin *Aurora* in Boston, MA under strict security. Ship sails at midnight.

» Sept 16: Day spent at sea.

» Sept 17: *Aurora* arrives in Bar Harbor, ME. Local population provides a grand welcome. Departs in the evening.

» Sept 18: *Aurora* arrives Halifax, Nova Scotia. Replacement crew and some stranded passengers embarked. Leaves for Southampton in the evening.

» Sept 24: After tracking south to avoid Hurricane Gabrielle, *Aurora* sights the South coast of England and proceeds up the English Channel.

» Sept 25: *Aurora* berths in Southampton.

KEY INSIGHTS

» The entertainment industry depends on the empowerment of people, especially for live performances.

» Performers need to adapt their material to the audience and the corporate requirements of the venue.

» In a crisis, empowered people are able to use their skills and initiative in a freer manner than those who are strictly controlled.

» Tight controls are often difficult in a crisis, hence the need to rely on empowered staff to make decisions quickly.

> » Job roles can change quickly, as happened to Aurora's entertainment staff – empowered people can deal with such changes.

CASE 3: TOYOTA

The original name of the company was Toyoda, but Toyota apparently requires fewer strokes when writing in Japanese.

Toyota is clearly a Japanese company, but in fact its vehicles are made in many parts of the world, begging the question as to whether a Toyota produced in the US is an American vehicle or one manufactured in the UK is British. Of course, some would say they are Japanese!

From humble beginnings in 1918 as the Toyoda Spinning and Weaving Company, Toyota has become a giant of the automobile industry. Its first vehicles were produced in 1936, but then the war intervened. Toyota was allowed to carry on trading after 1945 and in 1957 first exported its Crown model to the US.

The reason for choosing Toyota for this case study is the company philosophy of wanting an empowered workforce. Toyota does not believe in blame or punishment if the training and resources have been inadequate. This, as has already been shown in this material, is a key part of empowerment. Toyota's training is world class. Anybody starting a job with Toyota can expect to be well trained. They can also expect to be listened to if they have an idea and be rewarded for it.

The quality assurance system at Toyota relies on those manufacturing the product, thus giving them ownership. Toyota believes in the contribution of people for the long haul. Potential is not released overnight and employees need to see that they have a long-term future. Toyota was one of the pioneers of the Kanban, or Just in Time (JIT), and the Kaizen, or continuous improvement in quality systems. Working to such close time specifications and with a responsibility for both ensuring and improving quality requires employees who can react quickly, hence a need for the empowerment of the workforce. The control of production is ultimately in the hands of those directly involved in the manufacturing process.

There are good reasons for a company like Toyota to locate part of its manufacturing within its target markets. Customers can identify more closely with a local product and import restrictions can be avoided.

There are cultural difficulties to be overcome, however, but involving and empowering the workforce is a powerful method of overcoming any problems. There is no doubt that Toyota's move into Kentucky was initially viewed with suspicion, but the benefits to workers soon became apparent, especially as Toyota senior staff took time to understand the needs of the local community.

When Toyota bought a previously low performance US plant there was a fear amongst the workforce that the company had no long-term commitment. In a stroke of motivational genius, Toyota did not bother with long speeches, they repainted the plant (at a considerable cost) into a bright white.

Toyota supervisors are trained and encouraged to work with and facilitate staff rather than to control them. It is hardly surprising that Toyota is welcomed into new areas as a bringer of employment on a long-term basis and that their vehicles are of high quality. Quality and empowerment go together. Empower the staff and quality becomes their, rather than purely your, concern.

TIME LINE FOR TOYOTA

» 1918: Toyoda Spinning and Weaving commence operations.
» 1933: Automobile operation started.
» 1936: First vehicles produced. Trucks exported to China.
» 1937: Toyota Motor Co formed.
» 1957: Exports to US begin.
» 1958: First overseas plant in Brazil.
» 1984: Joint venture with General Motors.
» 1985: First US manufacturing plant opened.
» 1992: First UK manufacturing plant opened.

KEY INSIGHTS
Toyota

» Training is a key to empowerment.
» Supervisors should work with and facilitate employees.

» Nobody should be blamed for a mistake that occurs either because they were not trained or had insufficient resources.
» Empowered workers produce quality products.

Key Concepts and Thinkers

This chapter consists of the following:

» a glossary for empowerment; and
» information on key thinkers in the field of empowerment.

A GLOSSARY FOR EMPOWERMENT

Allowable weakness – A concept by Meredith Belbin. The negative side of a positive strength. If the weakness is corrected there is a danger that the strength will be diluted. In the same way as a coin cannot have just one side, allowable weaknesses are connected to the strength and must be managed, not eliminated.

Accountability – The obligation to ensure that certain tasks are carried out.

Authority – The use of legitimate power.

Blame culture – An organizational culture where blame and punishment are the main means of control.

Classical management – A traditional approach to management that stresses the controlling nature of management (see Scientific management, below).

Coaching – The managerial role concerned with working with members of staff to develop and empower them, and release their potential.

Contingency theory – A theory of management much used in contemporary literature to reflect the fact that there is no one right method of organizing and managing modern organizations, but that the methods used should be selected so as to be contingent with the situation at the particular time and place.

Culture – The values, attitudes, and beliefs ascribed to and accepted by a group, nation or organization. In effect, "the way we do things around here."

Delegation – Handing down responsibility together with the necessary resources and authority to somebody below one in the organization.

Empowerment – The process of releasing the full potential of employees in order for them to take on greater responsibility and authority in the decision-making process and providing the resources for this process to occur.

Glass ceiling – The invisible barrier beyond which women and minority groups often fail to pass when progressing up the organizational hierarchy.

Globalization – The integration of the global economy with the dismantling of trade barriers and the expanding political and economic power of multinational corporations.

Information and communication technology (ICT) – Technology related to the connection of computer and communications technology to produce a synergy (see below) between them. ICT was originally known as information technology (IT). However, more and more computer-type applications also involve communication with other computers or communication devices, hence the adoption of the acronym ICT.

Information overload – The result of having so much information that it is difficult to sort out the important from the trivial and the urgent from the less urgent. Modern technology has made this a major problem. Whilst computers can store and process information very quickly, the human brain requires more time.

Mechanistic empowerment – A concept by Spreitzer and Quinn. Empowerment that is driven by senior management instituting delegation etc. This type of empowerment could almost be described as pseudo-empowerment as considerable decision-making and control remains in the hand of management

Organic empowerment – A concept by Spreitzer and Quinn. This is true empowerment, that is a bottom up approach which begins with an understanding of employee needs and which uses team building to encourage cooperation and support. It is a process based on trust.

Organization – The structure set up as a human strategy for achieving a desired goal.

Power – The resource/force that drives influence. The sources of power within the work situation are: physical power, personality power (charisma), expertise, position power, resource power, and relationship power.

Responsibility – The obligation to actually carry out a task.

Scientific management – An early twentieth century concept proposed by F.W. Taylor in the US and based on the idea that work could be measured and rates set for the job. The concept assumes that money is the main motivator for work.

Simultaneous loose–tight properties – A term coined by Peters and Waterman to indicate that there are some functions that need tight control, but others where the staff should be empowered.

Span of control – the number of people it is traditionally assumed that one person can control (usually believed to be five or six in traditionally managed organizations). New technologies may be raising the limit. Above the span of control another hierarchical layer may be necessary.

Standard operating procedures (SOPs) – A set of laid-down rules and procedures for dealing with commonplace events in order to achieve consistency.

Synergy – A phenomenon where the sum of the parts is greater than the whole. A team of five working in synergy will produce the output of six.

Team roles – A person's tendency to behave in a certain way when working in a team situation (see also team role theory).

Team role theory – A concept pioneered by Meredith Belbin in the UK proposing that a successful team contains individuals who take up specific team roles based on personality in addition to their functional work roles (see also team roles).

Theory X – (McGregor)

» The average human being dislikes work and avoids working if at all possible.

» This dislike of work means that employees need to be controlled, directed and even threatened if necessary if the organization is to fulfill its objectives.

» People require direction but do not want responsibility.

Theory Y – (McGregor)

» Work is a natural human function.

» People relish responsibility.

» The rewards people seek are not only monetary.

» The intellectual and creative potential of most employees is under-utilized.

KEY THINKERS

All of the books referred to in this section are listed fully in Chapter 9.

Belbin, Meredith

Working from the 1980s onwards, Meredith Belbin proposed the concept of team roles and used it to study successful and unsuccessful teams. As covered earlier, teamwork is of vital importance to the entrepreneurial organization. His work was first used in the UK but has since spread throughout the world and is used in team building and as a recruitment aid by many organizations. The nine team roles that Belbin proposed need to be present in a team to ensure the necessary balance and synergy for effective performance. Thus diversity in team membership is to be welcomed and it is important that organizations achieve a diversity and balance between those in entrepreneurial roles and those whose work is more routine. Individuals can be tested for their preferred roles using a questionnaire and Belbin Associates' INTERPLACE® software. Belbin's later work has linked team role theory to organizational design.

There is more information on Belbin's work in *Managing Diversity*, another title in the ExpressExec series.

Highlights: books

» 1981: *Management Teams – Why they Succeed or Fail.*
» 1993: *Team Roles at Work.*
» 1996: *The Coming Shape of Organizations.*
» 2000: *Beyond the Team.*
» 2001: *Managing Without Power – Gender Relationships in the Story of Human Evolution.*

Highlights: other

» INTERPLACE® software for team role profiling.

Blanchard, Kenneth

Author and co-author of a large number of texts, Ken Blanchard is best known for the *One Minute Manager*® with Spencer Johnson, a text that must appear on nearly every business student's bookshelf and on those of many a CEO. Recognized by awards throughout the world, Blanchard has been an inspiration to those who seek empowerment and advancement. His work seeks to provide methods for both individuals and organizations to release potential in practical and insightful ways.

Now holding the position of "chief spiritual officer" of the Ken Blanchard companies, he is a visiting lecturer at Cornell University, where he is also trustee emeritus of the board of trustees.

A selection of Blanchard texts especially relevant to empowerment is given below.

Highlights: books

» 1985: *The One Minute Manager* (with Spencer Johnson).
» 1996: *Everyone's a Coach* (with Don Shula).
» 1998: *Empowerment Takes more than a Minute* (with John P. Carlos and Alan Randolph).
» 1999: *The 3 Keys to Empowerment* (with John P. Carlos and Alan Randolph).

Byham, William C.

William C. Byham is president and cofounder of Development Dimensions International (DDI), which specializes in aligning clients' people strategies with their business strategies.

An expert in several fields, Dr Byham began his business career as an innovator in the field of personnel assessment. As a manager of selection, appraisal, and management development for J.C. Penney, Byham was a pioneer in the field of assessment center methodologies, and developed his ideas about empowering leadership that would become the foundation of *Zapp!*. Later, as a consultant, Byham worked with some of the world's largest corporations, sharing insights on how to hire and develop the right people, and conveying his personal message of *Zapp!*. A visionary in employee and manager training, Byham's philosophies and techniques have touched the lives of millions of people. Today, Byham applies the principles of empowerment in dealing with the more than 1,000 employees of his Pittsburgh-based company. Despite the pressures imposed by rapid growth and international expansion, Byham keeps his employees happy by empowering them and making sure they love their jobs.

Byham is an internationally renowned speaker and has received numerous awards and citations, including Entrepreneur of the Year (1994) and CEO Communicator of the Year (1996).

Highlights: book

» 1999: *Zapp!: the Lightning of Empowerment* (with Jeff Cox).

Follett, Mary Parker

Mary Parker Follett was one of the early management writers but one whose ideas have stood the test of time. A political thinker as well as a management theorist, she had a vision of empowered citizens engaging in civic dialogue using neighborhood centers as their base. Such ideas hark back to Ancient Greece but are also echoed in modern ideas on devolution and empowerment. She was one of the first to see the link between management and governance. Her classic work is *The New State*, published in 1918. Living between 1868 and 1933, her experience ranged from the post-civil war US through to the Great Depression.

Highlights: book

» 1918: *The New State*.

Herzberg, Frederick Irving

Frederick Irving Herzberg, born in Lynn, MA, in 1923 became known internationally for his theories on motivating workers. His work focused on helping companies understand how to motivate workers and increase productivity. He is known for his Motivation-Hygiene Theory, which states that employers should provide a good working environment and decent pay and benefits. These things keep job dissatisfaction at a minimum, just as good hygiene and sanitation keep diseases at a minimum. These factors do not, however, motivate people but a lack of them acts to demotivate.

Herzberg stated that to motivate employees, employers must recognize them for their efforts, help them feel a sense of accomplishment and provide ways for them to advance in their careers.

Herzberg said employers over time should expand the responsibility, scope and challenge of their employees' jobs. He said this job enrichment increases motivation and productivity. The links to empowerment are obvious as empowerment is also about recognition and achievement.

He was a professor of management at Case Western Reserve University in Cleveland, where he created the Department of Industrial Mental Health before joining the University of Utah in 1976.

Highlights: book

» 1962: *Work and the Nature of Man* (Chapter 9).

Kanter, Rosabeth Moss

Rosabeth Moss Kanter is an internationally known business leader, educator and award-winning author. A professor at the Harvard Business School, she advises major corporations and governments worldwide, and is the author or co-author of over 300 articles and 13 books.

Considered one of the most prominent business speakers and strategy and change management consultants in the world, she has delivered the keynote address for trade associations, civic associations, and national conventions in nearly every State of the US and in over 20 countries. She also served as editor of *Harvard Business Review* from 1989–92, and was a finalist for a National Magazine Award for General Excellence in 1991.

Named one of the 100 most important women in America by the *Ladies' Home Journal* and one of the 50 most powerful women in the world by *The Times* of London, she has received 19 honorary doctoral degrees and over a dozen leadership awards. Her public service activities span local and global interests.

Rosabeth Moss Kanter is now one of the most important authorities on the management of change, a subject that has major implications for empowerment, as it is from empowered staff that the impetus for many changes come and it is those same staff who are often the most effective change agents.

Highlights: books

» 1985: *The Change Masters: Innovation and Entrepreneurship in the American Corporation*.
» 1992: *When Giants Learn to Dance*.
» 1992: *The Challenge of Organizational Change: How Companies Experience It and Leaders Guide It*.
» 1997: *World Class: Thriving Locally in the Global Economy*.
» 2001: *E-volve*.

Logan, David

A professor at the University of Southern California, Logan, together with ex-athlete John King, is a keen advocate of coaching as a component of empowerment.

There is nothing new about coaching. Its basic concepts have been around since human beings began competing in athletic contests etc. Athletes, especially, have used coaches to guide them through the process of transforming their potential into top performance. Logan points out that business managers face a similar problem i.e. getting maximum performance out of their employees. Logan believes that the payoff for becoming a manager-coach is clear: manager-coaches are more productive, their workplaces are more efficient, their people constantly develop their skills, and their companies' performances improve.

Highlights: book

» 2001: *The Coaching Revolution* (with John King).

McGregor, Douglas

Douglas McGregor was born in 1906 in Detroit. He attended Oberlin College and Wayne Universities, graduating from the latter in 1932. He received a PhD in experimental psychology from Harvard in 1935, carrying an A grade in every course.

On his graduation from Harvard after a break from studies to marry (he ended up as a gas station manager) he taught there for two years and then went to the Massachusetts Institute of Technology in 1937. He was the first full time teacher of psychology in that institution. His final role at MIT was Professor of Psychology and executive director of the Industrial Relations Section of MIT.

From 1939 Douglas McGregor served as consultant for a dozen industries and labor unions in the East and Mid West of the US. He is best known for his Theory X and Theory Y work, which, as shown in Chapter 5, is of critical importance to a study of empowerment.

Highlights: book

» 1960: *The Human Side of Enterprise*.

Murrell, Kenneth

Professor of management and management information systems at the University of West Florida, Murrell has worked with a large number of international organizations. His experiences led him to write *Empowering Employees* with Mimi Meredith, the owner of Wordsmiths Unlimited. A practical guide to the steps organizations must take, the work concentrates on the importance of dialog and the challenge for managers. A useful management styles survey assists managers in refining their own views and practice about management. Murrell makes the point that it is a survey, not a test. Attitudes can and do change with knowledge.

Highlights: book

» 2000: *Empowering Employees* (with Mimi Meredith).

Peters, Tom

From the publication of *In Search of Excellence* in 1982 onwards, Tom Peters has become one of the best-known names in the fields of management, change and quality. His message has been delivered on a global basis and has reached a huge audience, initially of senior but more recently including junior staff.

Three quotes express the importance Tom Peters has had on modern organizational thinking:

> "In no small part, what American corporations have become is what Peters has encouraged them to be."
>
> *The New Yorker*
>
> "Peters is . . . the father of the post-modern corporation."
>
> *Los Angeles Times*
>
> "We live in a Tom Peters world."
>
> *Fortune Magazine*

Tom Peters describes himself as a prince of disorder, champion of bold failures, maestro of zest, professional loudmouth, corporate cheerleader, and a lover of markets, *Fortune Magazine* has also referred to him as the Ur-guru (guru of gurus) of management and compares him to Ralph Waldo Emerson, Henry David Thoreau, and Walt Whitman. *The Economist* has titled him as the Über-guru (literally over-guru). His unconventional views led *Business Week* to describe him as business's best friend and worst nightmare. Best friend because of the challenges he throws out which, if taken up, can lead to success, and worst nightmare because his ideas have challenged conventional thinking – always an uncomfortable thing to do.

Tom followed up on the success of *In Search of Excellence* (1982, with Robert Waterman) with four more best-selling hardback books: *A Passion for Excellence* (1985, with Nancy Austin); *Thriving on Chaos* (1987); *Liberation Management* (1992 ... acclaimed as the "management book of the decade" for the 1990s); *The Circle of Innovation: You Can't Shrink Your Way to Greatness* (1997); and a pair of best-selling paperback originals, *The Tom Peters Seminar: Crazy Times Call for Crazy Organizations* (1993) and *The Pursuit of WOW!: Every Person's Guide to Topsy-Turvy Times* (1994). The first of Tom's series of books on reinventing work were released in September 1999: *The Brand You 50, The Project 50* (as an e-book, it knocked Stephen King out of 1st place on the e-best seller's list!) and *The Professional Service Firm 50*.

Tom Peters also presents about 100 major seminars globally each year. Organizations pay considerable sums for their staff to attend these seminars. He has also authored hundreds of articles for various newspapers and popular and academic journals, including *Business Week, The Economist*, the *Financial Times, The Wall Street Journal, The New York Times, Fast Company, The Washington Monthly, California Management Review, The Academy of Management Review, Forbes*, and *The Harvard Business Review*.

Tom Peters' philosophy for the re-invention of business and organizations is about change, giving power to people and encouraging entrepreneurship. He recognizes that we are in a changing, sometimes chaotic world and sees that as an opportunity, not a threat for organizations with the courage to move forward. The research for *In Search of Excellence* was under the auspices of the McKinley organization and was a review of excellent companies in the US and how America could re-establish its position in world trade. From those early ideas and the attributes contained within (see Chapter 6) has developed the Peters philosophy, a philosophy very much concerned with entrepreneurship.

Highlights: books

» 1982: *In Search of Excellence* (with Waterman, R.).
» 1985: *A Passion For Excellence* (with Austin, N.).

» 1989: *Thriving on Chaos*.
» 1992: *Liberation Management*.
» 1994: *The Pursuit of WOW!*
» 1997: *The Circle of Innovation*.
» 1999: *The Brand You 50*.
» 1999: *The Project 50*.
» 1999: *The Professional Service Firm 50*.

Quinn, Robert E.

A University of Michigan professor and author, Quinn has written over 30 books on organizations, change and empowerment. *A Company of Leaders*, with Gretchen M. Spreitzer, considers the five disciplines that are required to release (they use the term unleash, suggesting that it is something waiting to burst out) the potential of the work force.

One can do little more than quote Warren Bennis, professor at the University of Southern California, and a world authority on leadership, who has said that Quinn's 2000 book, *Change the World*, is one of the most significant books on personal and organizational transformation that he has read in some time.

Quinn believes that only through the empowerment of employees can a modern business be a success. He believes that empowered workers behave as though they were "owners" of the business and thus have a continuing vested interest in its success.

A selection of Quinn's work especially relevant to empowerment is given below.

Highlights: books

» 1988: *Beyond Rational Management*.
» 2000: *Change the World*.
» 2001: *A Company of Leaders* (with Gretchen M. Spreitzer).
» 2001: *Competency – Becoming a Master Manager*.

Trompenaars, Fons

Working originally in the Netherlands for Royal Dutch Shell, Fons Trompenaars has been one of the most influential writers on the management of cultural diversity. Shell as a global organization has considerable experience in managing diversity and Trompenaars set out to put these experiences into a conceptual framework that could be transferred to other organizations. It is hard to find work on cultural diversity within the work situation that does not cite Trompenaars.

His initial work – *Riding the Waves of Culture*, about understanding cultural diversity in business – was published in 1993 and was bought in large quantities by organizations such as British Airways, where it was required reading for the tutors employed on the management program detailed in the case study in Chapter 7. The book not only provided a contextual framework, but also provided concrete examples of the differing cultural norms that managers were likely to encounter and strategies for dealing with them in a sensitive and effective manner. The empowerment of those in different cultures has to be handled sensitively and it is Trompenaars' sound practical advice on achieving this that makes his work so useful and important.

In association with Charles Hampden-Turner, Trompenaars looked in more detail at the competencies required for cross-cultural management (*Building Cross Cultural Competence*) and the requirements for twenty-first century business leaders in a more globalized environment (*21 Leaders for the 21st Century*) as well as a detailed examination of social, cultural and economic differences between Asia and the West in *Mastering the Infinite Game*.

Fons Trompenaars is recommended reading for all those dealing with cultural issues within the workplace, blending as he does practical advice within a useful conceptual framework.

Highlights: books

» 1997: *Riding the Waves of Culture*.
» 1997: *Mastering the Infinite Game* (with C. Hampden-Turner).
» 2000: *Building Cross Cultural Competence* (with C. Hampden-Turner).
» 2001: *21 Leaders for the 21st Century* (with C. Hampden-Turner).

Resources

This chapter lists resource material relevant to empowerment:

» books;
» journals; and
» Websites.

BOOKS

Ardrey, R. (1967) *The Territorial Imperative*. Collins, London.

Belbin, M.R. (1981) *Management Teams – Why they Succeed or Fail*. Heinemann, Oxford.

Belbin, M.R. (1993) *Team Roles at Work*. Butterworth Heinemann, Oxford.

Belbin, M.R. (1996) *The Coming Shape of Organizations*. Butterworth Heinemann, Oxford.

Belbin, M.R. (2000) *Beyond the Team*. Butterworth Heinemann, Oxford.

Belbin, M.R. (2001) *Managing Without Power – Gender Relationships in the Story of Human Evolution*. Butterworth Heinemann, Oxford.

Blanchard, K. and Johnson, S. (1985) *The One Minute Manager*. HarperCollins, New York.

Blanchard, K. and Shula, D. (1996) *Everyone's a Coach*. Zondervan Publishing, Grand Rapids, MI.

Blanchard, K. Carlos, J.P. and Randolph, A. (1998) *Empowerment Takes more than a Minute*. Berrett-Koehler, San Francisco.

Blanchard, K., Carlos, J.P. and Randolph, A. (1999) *The 3 Keys to Empowerment*. Berrett-Koehler, San Francisco.

Byham, W.C. and Cox, J. (1998) *Zapp!: The Lightning of Empowerment*. Random House, New York.

Cartwright, R. (2001) *Mastering the Business Environment*. Palgrave, Basingstoke.

Clarke, R.D. (2001) "Excellence by the Graham." *Black Enterprise*, September 2001, Vol. 32 No. 2 pp. 78–87.

Davidson, M. and Cooper, G. (1992) *Shattering the Glass Ceiling*. Paul Chapman, London.

Drummond, H. (1992) *Power – Creating it, Using it*. Kogan Page, London.

Ellwood, W. (2001) *The No-nonsense Guide to Globalization*. New Internationalist, Oxford.

Fayol, H. (1916) *General and Industrial Administration*. Translated from the French by Storrs, C. (1949). Pitman, London.

Fiedler, F. (1964) *A Theory of Leadership Effectiveness*. McGraw Hill, New York.

Follett, M.P. (1918) *The New State*. Latest edition 1998, Penn State University Press, Philadelphia.

Ginnodo, W. (1997) *The Power of Empowerment*. Pride Publications, Arlington Height, IL.

Gray, John (1992) *Men are from Mars, Women are from Venus*. HarperCollins, New York.

Handy, C. (1976) *Understanding Organizations*. Penguin, London.

Handy, C. (1978) *Gods of Management*. Souvenir Press, London.

Hastings, M. and Jenkins, S. (1983) *The Battle for the Falklands*. Michael Joseph, London.

Harris, P.R. and Moran, R.T. (2000) *Managing Cultural Differences*. Gulf Publishing Co., Houston, TX.

Herzberg, F. (1962) *Work and the Nature of Man*. World Publishing, New York.

Kanter, R.M. (1985) *The Change Masters: Innovation and Entrepreneurship in the American Corporation*. Free Press, New York.

Kanter, R.M. (1992) *When Giants Learn to Dance*. International Thomson Business Press, New York.

Kanter, R.M. (1992) *The Challenge of Organizational Change: How Companies Experience It and Leaders Guide It*. Free Press, New York.

Kanter, R.M. (1997) *World Class: Thriving Locally in the Global Economy*. Simon & Schuster, New York.

Kanter, R.M. (2001) *E-volve*. Harvard Business School Press, Cambridge, MA.

Lewis, R.D. (2000) *When Cultures Collide*. Nicholas Brealey, London.

Logan, D. and King, J. (2001) *The Coaching Revolution*. Adams Media Corporation, Holbrook, MA.

Maslow, A. (1970) *Motivation and Personality*. Harper & Row, New York.

McGregor, D. (1960) *The Human Side of Enterprise*. McGraw-Hill, New York.

Morris, D. (1969) *The Human Zoo*. Jonathon Cape, London.

Murrell, K.L. and Meredith, M. (2000) *Empowering Employees*. McGraw-Hill, New York.

Nicolson, N. (2000) *Managing the Human Animal*. Crown, New York.

Nicolson, N. and Nicholson, J. (2000) *A1*. Collins, London.

Peter L.J. and Hull, R. (1969) *The Peter Principle*. William Morrow, New York.

Peters, T. and Waterman, R. (1982) *In Search of Excellence*. Harper & Row, New York.

Peters, T. and Austin, N. (1994) *A Passion For Excellence*. Harper-Collins, New York.

Peters, T. (1989) *Thriving on Chaos*. HarperCollins, New York.

Peters, T. (1992) *Liberation Management*. Alfred A. Knopf, New York.

Peters, T. (1995) *The Pursuit of WOW!* Random House, New York.

Peters, T. (1997) *The Circle of Innovation*. Hodder & Stoughton, New York.

Peters, T. (1999) *The Brand You 50*. Alfred A. Knopf, New York.

Peters, T. (1999) *The Project 50*. Alfred A. Knopf, New York.

Peters, T. (1999) *The Professional Service Firm 50*. Alfred A. Knopf, New York.

Pitt, B. (1962) *1918 – The Last Act*. Cassell, London.

Quinn, R.E. (1988) *Beyond Rational Management*. Jossey-Bass Wiley, San Francisco.

Quinn, R.E. (1996) *Deep Change*. Jossey-Bass Wiley, San Francisco.

Quinn, R.E. (2000) *Change the World – How Ordinary People Can Achieve Extraordinary Results*. Jossey-Bass, San Francisco.

Quinn, R.E. (2001) *Competence – Becoming a Master Manager*. John Wiley, New York.

Quinn, R.E. and Spreitzer, G. (2001) *A Company of Leaders – Five Disciplines for Unleashing the Power in Your Workforce*. Jossey-Bass, San Francisco.

Stith, A. (1998) *Breaking the Glass Ceiling – Sexism and Racism in Corporate America*. Warwick, New York.

Price, C. (2000) *The Internet Entrepreneurs*. Pearson Education, Harlow.

Taylor, F.W. (1911) *Principles of Scientific Management*. Harper, New York.

Trompenaars, F. (1993) *Riding the Waves of Culture*. Economist Books, London.

Trompenaars, F. (1997) *Mastering the Infinite Game* (with C. Hampden-Turner). Capstone, Oxford.

Trompenaars, F. (2000) *Building Cross Cultural Competence* (with C. Hampden-Turner). Nicolas Brealey, London.

Trompenaars, F. (2001) *21 Leaders for the 21st Century* (with C. Hampden-Turner). Capstone, Oxford.

Wirth, L. (2000) *Breaking through the Glass Ceiling*. International Labor Organization, Geneva.

United Nations (1999) *Human Development Report*. UN Development Program/Oxford University Press, Oxford.

Urwick, L. (1947) *The Elements of Administration*. Pitman, London.

For information on Stephen Hawking and a sample selection of his books

Hawking, J. (1999) *Music to Move the Stars – a life with Stephen*. Macmillan, Basingstoke.

Hawking, S. (1988) *A Brief History of Time*, Bantam, Toronto/London.

Krauss, L. (1997) *The Physics of Star Trek*. Flamingo, London. Foreword by Stephen Hawking.

For information about Marriott Hotels

Marriott, J.R. Jnr and Brown, K.A. (1997) *The Spirit to Serve – Marriott's Way*. Harper, New York.

For information about Mary Kay

Gross, D. (1996) *Forbes Greatest Business Stories of All Time*. John Wiley & Sons, New York.

For information about P&O and the cruise industry

Cartwright, R. and Baird, C. (1999) *The Development and Growth of the Cruise Industry*. Butterworth Heinemann, Oxford.

Dawson, P. (1997) *Canberra – In the Wake of a Legend*. Conway Maritime Press/P&O Cruises, London.

Dickinson, R. and Vladimir, A. (1997) *Selling the Sea*. Wiley, New York.

P&O Cruises (2000) *Aurora – The Dawn of a New Era*. P&O Cruises, London.

P&O Cruises (1995) *Oriana – From Dream to Reality*. P&O Cruises, London.

Ward, D. (2000) *The Berlitz Guide to Cruising and Cruise Ships 2001*. Berlitz, Princeton, NJ.

For information about Toyota

Besser, T.L. (1996) *Team Toyota: Transplanting the Toyota Culture to the Camry Plant in Kentucky* (Suny Series in the Sociology of Work). State University of New York Press, New York.

Fujimoto, T. (1999) *The Evolution of Manufacturing Systems at Toyota*. OUP, New York.

Monden, Y. (1996) *The Toyota Management System: Linking the Seven Key Functional Areas*. Productivity Press, Portland, OR.

Lu, D.J. (1989) *Kanban, Just in Time at Toyota*. Productivity Press, Portland, OR.

JOURNALS, ETC.

The American Management Association (AMA)

The world's leading membership-based management development organization, the AMA offers a full range of business education and management development programs for individuals and organizations in Europe, the Americas and Asia. Through a variety of seminars and conferences, assessments and customized learning solutions, books and on-line resources, more than 700,000 AMA members and customers a year learn superior business skills and best management practices from a faculty of top practitioners. The on-line facilities offer access to a wide range of articles including issues related to empowerment.

Management Today

Institute of Management in the UK, monthly to members or by subscription. Often contains useful articles on issues concerned with empowerment.

Black Enterprise

A US magazine that aims to assist the financial empowerment of African Americans. It presents financial information and profiles successful African Americans. The magazine is, however, of use to all interested in empowerment as many of the issues it covers are applicable to all those seeking to release their potential.

Black Enterprise is published monthly in New York by Earl G. Graves Publishing and is also available on-line – see list of Websites at the end of this chapter.

Cross Cultural Letter to International Managers

Published 10 times a year by Richard Lewis Publications. See www.crossculture.com.

Fast Company

A US publication that features successful individuals and companies. Empowerment is a key theme of the magazine, which is published monthly out of Boston, MA. The magazine provides a practitioner rather than an academic approach.

Harvard Business Review

Leading business and management resource. Read worldwide and features contributions by the leading names in business and management. Published 10 times a year and available by subscription.

HR Magazine

An HR magazine covering a wide range of US human resource issues and published by the Society for Human Resource Management in Alexandria, VA.

Human Resource Management International Digest

A digest of useful HR articles from many sources gathered on a global basis and published seven times a year. Available on subscription.

International Journal of Human Resource Management

A journal that is concerned with strategic human resource management and future trends in a global environment. Published eight times a year by Routledge and available on subscription.

Organizational Behavior and Human Decision Processes

Published in San Diego by Academic Press Inc. for a global academic market, this journal is concerned with organizational behavior, organizational psychology, and human cognition, judgment, and decision-making, hence its relevance to empowerment. The journal features articles that present original empirical research, theory development, literature reviews, and methodological advancements relevant to the areas above. Topics covered include perception, attitudes, emotion, well-being, motivation, choice, and performance.

People Management

Magazine of the UK Chartered Institute of Personnel and Training (CIPD). Contains articles on all aspects of personnel and training with especial relevance to the UK. Available by subscription and published every two weeks.

WEBSITES

Useful information can be found at the following Websites:

www.academicpress.com/obhdp

Organizational Behavior and Human Decision Processes Website.

www.amanet.org

American Management Association Website.

www.belbin.com

Website for Meredith Belbin.

www.blackenterprise.com

Black Enterprise Website.

www.crossculture.com

Website for Richard D. Lewis.

www.fastcompany.com

Fast Company magazine Website.

www.hbsp.harvard.edu/products/hbr

Website for Harvard Business Review.

www.hawking.org.uk

Website for Stephen Hawking.

www.inst-mgt.org.uk

Institute of Management (UK) Website.

www.marriott.com

Marriott Hotels Website.

www.emeraldinsight.com/hrmid.htm

Human Resource Management International Digest Website.

www.shrm.org

HR Magazine Website.

www.tandf.co.uk/journals/routledge/09585192.html

International Journal of Human Resource Management Website.

www.peoplemanagement.co.uk

People Management magazine Website.

www.poprincesscruises.com

P&O Princess Cruises Website.

www.toyota.com

Toyota Website.

Ten Steps to Empowerment

This chapter contains 10 steps to assist the empowerment process.

1 Empower yourself.
2 Look for potential.
3 Communicate the vision and goals.
4 Catch people in not out - engender trust.
5 Listen to the employees - give credit where credit is due.
6 Support and security.
7 More facilitation - less control.
8 Simultaneous loose–tight properties.
9 Provide resources.
10 Be a coach.

1. EMPOWER YOURSELF

It is very difficult to even consider the empowerment of subordinates unless one is empowered oneself. Whilst complete empowerment involves others, a knowledge of one's own abilities and limitations is liberating.

In order to empower employees, a manager has to feel confident in his or her self. A diffident manager will soon pass his or her lack of confidence on to the workforce and they will feel wary about empowerment if working under such a person. They may well feel that such a manager will use empowerment as a means to pass on any problems to others. This type of behavior has no place in empowerment.

Many managers feel threatened by empowerment as they feel that it will expose their vulnerabilities, but if they are empowered themselves they should see that empowerment is a positive step and that they will also be beneficiaries.

2. LOOK FOR POTENTIAL

Empowerment is not about having the work done by somebody else. It is about releasing the potential of staff. It is difficult to find a person who has no potential – the old adage that "there is good and bad in everybody" is very apt.

Potential needs a nurturing environment to germinate and grow. One of the key tasks of a manager is to provide such an environment. Releasing potential benefits both the individual and the organization. The manager may need to assist with training, job enrichment, new opportunities, and be a sounding board for ideas. He or she will also need to be a coach (see later).

Potential may often be hidden by shyness, diffidence, or a lack of confidence. It is the manager's job to get behind the public façade of a person and try to discover the true potential that lies behind it. The work of Meredith Belbin (Chapter 6 and Chapter 8) suggests that every weakness has a positive strength attached to it; hence the term "allowable weakness." The Belbin studies also suggest that different personality types will have different strengths and thus potential. The manager's responsibility is to work with the employee to recognize and release his or her potential.

3. COMMUNICATE THE VISION AND GOALS

It is a feature of human behavior that people need direction. The vision and goals of an organization, properly formulated and communicated, can provide a sense of direction that promotes empowerment. If people can see how their job fits into the wider scheme of things, they will be more efficient.

Direction should not be so prescriptive as to restrict flexibility. One of the main reasons for empowering staff is to allow them to make decisions and respond flexibly. If they have a clear view of what the organization is aiming for, they can ensure that their decisions will lead to results that help achieve the organizational goals.

4. CATCH PEOPLE IN NOT OUT – ENGENDER TRUST

Too many managers spend their time trying to catch people out. This is both unproductive and a waste of energy. The manager wastes his or her energy looking for small infractions amongst the majority of things people are doing right, and the staff devote energy to covering up mistakes that, if discussed openly, could lead to greater efficiency.

Whenever managers adopt a policing role rather than a coaching one, they engender distrust and create a "them and us" situation that is not conducive to good decision-making.

If a person shows that they cannot be trusted, then steps must be taken to find out whether this is a fault of the work situation or the personality of the person concerned. If the former, then the manager has a responsibility to rectify matters; if the latter, then disciplinary action may well be appropriate.

Catching people in is more fun for all concerned as it leads to praise rather than punishment and encourages good work habits. There is no reason why work cannot be enjoyable. According to Theory Y (see Chapter 2), work is an integral part of human existence and thus should contain a fair element of pleasure.

5. LISTEN TO THE EMPLOYEES – GIVE CREDIT WHERE CREDIT IS DUE

Toyota managers and supervisors (see Chapter 7) are encouraged to listen to employees. As educational standards rise, employees can often analyze situations with a high degree of competence. The person actually carrying out a task is usually the best person to comment on ways of improving procedures.

If a good suggestion has come from an employee, the manager should ensure that the employee receives the credit. Monetary rewards are often not necessary – praise given in front of peers is a great motivator, as it provides recognition. The manager should never try to take credit him- or herself – that will ensure that suggestions dry up. The recognition for the manager is in showing that he or she listens and acts on the ideas of others.

Even if the suggestion is impractical, praise should still be given for thinking about the task – that will encourage the employee to continue seeking improvements. Sarcasm or putting the employee down should never be used, as this is the fastest method for ensuring that suggestions dry up.

6. SUPPORT AND SECURITY

Empowerment can be a threat to employees. They need to be assured that management will support them. The notions of accountability and responsibility are important. Most employees are used to being responsible but accountability may be a new concept.

If the organization has had a blame culture in operation, people will have learnt to suppress their potential for fear of punishment.

Support needs to include training and development activities. In an empowered organization the divisions between workers and managers become very blurred, hence the need for some form of management development for all staff.

If people feel secure and supported, managers will find that releasing potential becomes a much more natural process. If staff feel that they can speak out and be listened to (see above), they will be far more likely to assist in the running of the organization rather than just carrying out the tasks allocated to them.

7. MORE FACILITATION – LESS CONTROL

Facilitating managers are vital for the empowerment process. Controls, whilst necessary, should only be in place where relevant (see step 8 below). Facilitation is a partnership activity rather than the one-way process of control.

Facilitation is about the provision of direction and assistance rather than just giving orders. Whilst many managers believe that it is their job to keep tight controls on everything within their area of work, as will be shown in step 8, control should only be used where appropriate. If potential is to be released through empowerment, then controls need to be relaxed in order to provide the "room for people to grow."

8. SIMULTANEOUS LOOSE – TIGHT PROPERTIES

This famous phrase from Tom Peters and Bob Waterman (1982) indicates that there are times when controls are needed and others when they are not. Financial procedures, safety, personnel issues related to discrimination and above all quality requirements are issues that should be kept under tight control. Note that it is the setting of the minimum acceptable quality standard that should be controlled. The achieving of that standard is best left to an empowered staff. Organizational intervention should only be required if standards slip. However, an empowered team is likely to have dealt with any quality issues long before they come to the attention of senior management. One of the advantages of an empowered team is that it becomes self-policing. This alone can release management time and energy for more productive purposes.

9. PROVIDE RESOURCES

There is no point in telling people that they are empowered unless they have the resources available to make decisions and act upon them.

Resources do not only include tangible materials but also training, authority (the power to act) and financial freedom within the organizational budgeting and monetary control processes.

Managers who hang on to resources are in effect employing resource power (see Chapter 2) and not really empowering staff. In cases like this, empowerment becomes a sham and employees are likely to become frustrated and disillusioned.

10. BE A COACH

Managers who wish to empower staff need to add coaching to their range of skills.

Coaching (and associated mentoring) are not innate skills and the manager will need to undertake his or her training and development. Organizations that embark on empowerment are advised to ensure that their managers receive the necessary training and development so that they can carry out their coaching role.

Coaching requires a different relationship between manager and employee and there may well be both managers and employees who feel uncomfortable with the redefined relationship. Support and sensitivity will need to be available for both parties.

KEY LEARNING POINTS

» Managers who wish to empower should first empower themselves.

» It is rare that a member of staff has no or little potential. They might not recognize their own potential but their managers should seek it out.

» Empowerment requires that the organization communicates its vision and goals.

» Catching people in not out engenders trust.

» Managers should listen to the employees and give credit where credit is due.

» Empowered employees need support and security from management.

» More facilitation and less control is a feature of empowerment.

» Control only what should be controlled (simultaneous loose – tight properties).

» Without the provision of resources, empowerment is doomed. Do not exercise resource power.

» Empowered staff need coaching as well as managing.

Frequently Asked Questions (FAQs)

Q1: What is empowerment?

A: Empowerment is the process of releasing the full potential of employees in order for them to take on greater responsibility and authority in the decision-making process and providing the resources for this process to occur.

You can read more about definitions of empowerment in Chapter 2.

Q2: Why is empowerment such an important matter for organizations?

A: Empowerment releases the potential of employees and directs it towards organizational goals. Empowered employees are able to take decisions both at the point of work and nearer to the customer interface.

The importance of empowerment is covered in Chapter 3, Chapter 6 and Chapter 7.

Q3: Are the weaknesses displayed by some people just too great to empower them?

A: If a member of staff is so weak as to have no potential for empowerment, one might wish to question whether they should have been hired or promoted in the first place. However, for most people there is often a tendency to consider weaknesses rather than strengths. The work of Meredith Belbin, covered in Chapter 6 and Chapter 8, suggests that many weaknesses are allowable as they are the opposite side of a positive strength. Belbin's work also suggests that the strengths and thus the potential of different personality types differ.

Q4: Has information and communication technology (ICT) including the Internet aided empowerment?

A: By increasing access to information and education, and by freeing people from the constraints of geography, family, etc., ICT has major implications for empowerment. People who may not have been able to work because of where they live, having a young family or a disability can be empowered by ICT.

There is more about the ICT/Internet implications for empowerment in Chapter 5.

Q5: Surely managers need to control their areas of responsibility?

A: There are certain areas of any organization's activities that need to be controlled including financial procedures, safety, personnel issues related to discrimination, and quality requirements. However, in an empowered organization staff can be intimately involved with the control mechanisms. There are many areas of work where empowered staff and teams should be able to take their own decisions.

This is covered in greater detail in Chapter 6.

Q6: What is meant by power?

A: Power, as defined in the everyday world, is the resource that drives things. Anything that "gets something done" possesses this force known as power. Thus, money can be a form of power, as can expertise, information and knowledge. Money, information etc. are often referred to in management and business texts as resources, so it follows that power is a resource as well. Whilst there is often talk about the misuse of power it must be remembered that resources are neutral and it is up to the individual to decide how a resource is to be used. Power is covered in greater detail in Chapter 2.

Q7: Is empowerment a new idea?

A: It is not a new idea, but it only really gained currency from the 1970s onwards. Prior to then, control type classical management theories held sway. The latest ideas center around a contingency approach i.e. using a style of management appropriate to the situation

The evolution of empowerment is covered in Chapter 3.

Q8: What is the difference between authority, delegation, accountability and responsibility?

A:

» Authority is the legitimate use of power.
» Delegation refers to the handing down of the responsibility and resources to carry out a task whilst retaining accountability – it is not empowerment, but a step on the way to it.
» Accountability is the obligation to ensure that something is done, but does not mean that the accountable person has to actually do it.
» Responsibility is the obligation to do something as instructed etc.

Accountability cannot be delegated whereas responsibility can.

These issues are explored in Chapter 2.

Q9: How does the management role change when empowerment is employed?

A: The manager becomes much more of a coach and facilitator in an empowered organization. This is likely to produce training and development needs for both the manager and his or her staff.

Q10: Where are resources available to assist in understanding the process of empowerment?

A: A list of books, journals and Web addresses will be found in Chapter 9 and a glossary and details of key authorities in Chapter 8.

Index